THE
ADVENT
MISSION

The Seedbed Daily Text

+ THE
ADVENT
MISSION

Advent

OMAR RIKABI

Unless otherwise indicated, all Scripture quotations are taken from the Holy Bible, New Living Translation, copyright © 1996, 2004, 2015 by Tyndale House Foundation. Used by permission of Tyndale House Publishers, Inc., Carol Stream, Illinois 60188. All rights reserved.

Scripture quotations marked NIV are taken from the Holy Bible, New International Version®, NIV® Copyright © 1973, 1978, 1984, 2011 by Biblica, Inc.™ Used by permission of Zondervan. All rights reserved worldwide. www.zondervan.com The "NIV" and "New International Version" are trademarks registered in the United States Patent and Trademark Office by Biblica, Inc.™ All rights reserved worldwide.

Scripture quotations marked MSG are taken from *THE MESSAGE*, copyright © 1993, 1994, 1995, 1996, 2000, 2001, 2002 by Eugene H. Peterson. Used by permission of NavPress. All rights reserved. Represented by Tyndale House Publishers, Inc.

Printed in the United States of America

Cover and page design by Strange Last Name
Page layout by PerfecType, Nashville, Tennessee

Rikabi, Omar.
    The Advent mission / Omar Rikabi. – Frankin, Tennessee : Seedbed Publishing, ©2018.

        pages ; cm. (The Seedbed daily text)

        ISBN 9781628246131 (paperback)
        ISBN 9781628246148 (Mobi)
        ISBN 9781628246155 (ePub)
        ISBN 9781628246162 (uPDF)

        1. Advent--Meditations. 2. Devotional calendars. I. Title.
        II. Seedbed daily text.

BV40.R54 2018   242.33   2018954925

SEEDBED PUBLISHING
Franklin, Tennessee
seedbed.com

For my daughters,
Sadie, Norah, and Lilly,
"Daddy loves you as big as outer space!"

And in memory of Kelly Roach,
"I'll see you again
when the stars fall from the sky
and the moon turns red . . ."

Contents

Introduction
A New Mission

NASA's Apollo 13 had one mission: land on the moon. On April 13, 1971, the spacecraft carrying three astronauts was half way to the moon when an oxygen tank exploded. Now tumbling through space while leaking breathable air, losing power, and drifting off course, Commander Jim Lovell radioed to mission control: "Houston, we've had a problem," and their mission immediately changed. It was now a rescue mission, and the goal was to get back to Earth alive.

After they splashed down in the Pacific Ocean four days later, their mission was dubbed "the successful failure" because they lost their original goal of landing on the moon but made it back to Earth alive.

Our story begins with a simple mission: "The LORD God placed the man in the Garden of Eden to tend and watch over it" (Gen. 2:15).

But soon there was the big lie, rebellion, and so *Eden, we've had a problem*.

Now God had a new mission: save us from our sin and its catastrophic effects. It is a succesful failure because we lost our original creation goal, but God has succeeded in saving us through Jesus Christ.

The meaning of the word *mission* is "a sending; a charge to go and perform a specific duty." This leads us to the mission statement of Scripture, John 3:16–17: "For God so loved the world that he gave his one and only Son, that whoever believes in him shall not perish but have eternal life. For God did not send his Son into the world to condemn the world, but to save the world through him."

This time of year we go straight to Christmas, the first part of the mission. But what about Advent, which is the last part of the mission? The first stage is Jesus' arrival in the manger. The final stage is his arrival in the clouds.

Maybe we lose sight of the real meaning of Advent because, for many of us, Advent is the launching pad to Christmas morning: a twenty-four-day countdown to stockings and presents. We don't think about Advent as first being about the second coming. After all, it's been two millennia since Christ was born, crucified, rose from the dead, ascended into heaven, and sent the Holy Spirit. And for two thousand years, we've been living somewhere between forgetting about or fretting over his return.

In his book *Give Them Christ*, Stephen Seamands writes, "the second coming should therefore not cause us to abandon this world or look for an escape from its suffering and evil. Instead, it should move us to become passionately and actively engaged in it."[1]

---

1. Stephen Seamands, *Give Them Christ: Preaching His Incarnation, Crucifixion, Resurrection, Ascension and Return* (Downers Grove, IL: Intervarsity Press, 2012), 176.

Preparing for that kind of Advent before we celebrate Christmas is how we get in on God's rescue mission. Consider these devotionals a launch manual for our mission together.

To get started, maybe we need to add a line to the mystery of our faith, which is really our mission hope: *Christ was born. Christ has died. Christ is risen. Christ will come again!*

Let the countdown begin . . .

+
THE
ADVENT
MISSION

Happy New Year

ROMANS 13:11–14 | This is all the more urgent, for you know how late it is; time is running out. Wake up, for our salvation is nearer now than when we first believed. The night is almost gone; the day of salvation will soon be here. So remove your dark deeds like dirty clothes, and put on the shining armor of right living. Because we belong to the day, we must live decent lives for all to see. Don't participate in the darkness of wild parties and drunkenness, or in sexual promiscuity and immoral living, or in quarreling and jealousy. Instead, clothe yourself with the presence of the Lord Jesus Christ. And don't let yourself think about ways to indulge your evil desires.

Consider This

Do you remember New Year's 2000? I sort of do. I'm not one for New Year's Eve parties. In fact, I would rather go to bed before midnight and wake up in a new year. But this was the arrival of a new millennium! The entire earth was celebrating this historic moment in space and time across the globe, and I was all alone.

All of my plans had fallen through, so I sat by myself at home watching the news show fireworks and celebrations as the clock struck midnight across each time zone, from the Great Pyramids in Egypt to the Statue of Liberty in New York.

When the new millennium arrived for me in Dallas, I drank too much champagne . . . more out of depression than celebration. More than a new year, it was a new era, and this was how I was starting out my resolutions to do things different: by getting a hangover. Instead of celebrating, I got disoriented.

Like many of us, I look to New Year's as a time to start over, because "this year is going to be better." But when we try to do it all in one day—in the midst of a frantic holiday season—we wake up still lost and disoriented, having given up on our resolutions by the end of the week.

Instead of a single day, we need a season. We need Advent.

We need Advent because it takes time for reorientation: to prepare, to repent, and to wake up to all that Christmas morning aspires to be. Advent is not a season to get lost in earthly celebration, but to be found in what God has done, is doing, and will do through Jesus Christ in a disoriented world.

Advent is New Year's for the church: the first season in the Christian calendar. Advent means "the arrival of a notable person, thing, or event." For Christians, it marks the celebration of the arrival of Jesus Christ, but not in the ways we often think of in the midst of mistletoe and holly.

In the Christian calendar, the end is the beginning. Before we celebrate Jesus' silent-night first arrival in the manger, we prepare for his trumpet-blasting second coming in the clouds. He will come back and bring history to a close, and we don't need to be afraid. Because as we'll see this season, his return is a good thing.

The earth has completed another trek around the sun, finishing its four seasons and preparing to make another orbit. Where will we find ourselves this year? Advent is an alternate to New Year's as an opportunity to let the church's seasons, not the world's, set the orbit for our lives.

CHRIST WAS BORN. CHRIST HAS DIED. CHRIST IS RISEN. CHRIST WILL COME AGAIN!

The Good Earth

2

GENESIS 1:1–10 | In the beginning God created the heavens and the earth. The earth was formless and empty, and darkness covered the deep waters. And the Spirit of God was hovering over the surface of the waters.

Then God said, "Let there be light," and there was light. And God saw that the light was good. Then he separated the light from the darkness. God called the light "day" and the darkness "night."

And evening passed and morning came, marking the first day.

Then God said, "Let there be a space between the waters, to separate the waters of the heavens from the waters of the earth." And that is what happened. God made this space to separate the waters of the earth from the waters of the heavens. God called the space "sky."

And evening passed and morning came, marking the second day.

Then God said, "Let the waters beneath the sky flow together into one place, so dry ground may appear." And that is what happened. God called the dry ground "land" and the waters "seas." And God saw that it was good.

Consider This

On Christmas Eve 1968, the crew of Apollo 8 became the first humans to orbit the moon. That evening, during the most-watched television event at the time, they sent back the first live images of Earth. At the end of the broadcast the three astronauts took turns reading today's text from Genesis, and ended with, "And from the crew of Apollo 8, we close with good night, good luck, a Merry Christmas—and God bless all of you, all of you on the good Earth."

It was an appropriate text for the first glimpse of our planet from the heavens, and the image was aptly titled, "Earth-Rise."

But we know what happened next in the Genesis story: mission failure.

God created humanity in his image, but we turned away in fear and rebellion, and all of creation still suffers. When we look at the world today, we see this isn't the way it was supposed to be: Floods. Cancer. Mass shootings. Sexual assault. Terrorism. War. Hunger. Anxiety. Depression. And on and on.

But remember, in the beginning it was the *good* earth, and that's what Advent is about: the final stage of the new mission God began after humanity fell. We get that Jesus was born, crucified, and is risen . . . but we often lose sight that he's also enthroned in heaven, interceding for the world, and will one day return to make all things new again.

Advent helps us see his mission and get in on it.

One of the Apollo 8 astronauts, Bill Anders, said they had prepared to explore the moon, but ended up discovering Earth.[2] That's what's needed here: a new way to see the earth. Theologically speaking, we need the Google Earth view, if you will. In our day-to-day lives, we spend most of our time on Google Street View, seeing only what's right in front of us. Our day-to-day view tends to be more oriented by the darkness of the world around us than by God's love for it.

Part of the reason we may not be ready for the return of Jesus is because we've not yet fully embraced the view of "For this is how God loved *the world:* He gave his one and only Son" (John 3:16, emphasis mine), where Jesus is ahead of us, present now through the Holy Spirit, working out the restoration of the whole world.

As the psalmist says:

> For your unfailing love is as high as the heavens.
>> Your faithfulness reaches to the clouds.
> Be exalted, O God, above the highest heavens.
>> May your glory shine over all the earth. (Ps. 57:10–11)

So then, Advent is a reorientation that refuses to only look at the street view but is first pulling back to see all that

---

2. Nasa Content Administrator, "Apollo 8: Christmas at the Moon," December 19, 2014, www.nasa.gov/topics/history/features/apollo_8.html.

God is doing to redeem *all* people's stories into his great divine story through Jesus Christ. It gives us the opportunity to pause and take inventory—to start with the end in mind and see if our lives look like our beliefs and prayers—so that Jesus' kingdom can come on earth as it is in heaven.

CHRIST WAS BORN. CHRIST HAS DIED. CHRIST IS RISEN. CHRIST WILL COME AGAIN!

3 The Reason for the Season(s)

JOHN 1:1–5 | In the beginning the Word already existed.
The Word was with God,
and the Word was God.
He existed in the beginning with God.
God created everything through him,
and nothing was created except through him.
The Word gave life to everything that was created,
and his life brought light to everyone.
The light shines in the darkness,
and the darkness can never extinguish it.

Consider This

Today I'd like to settle the "Jesus is the reason for the season" kerfuffle.

Previously, I shared the story of the Apollo 8 astronauts reading the creation story from Genesis 1 as they orbited the moon. They said they chose this text because it would be safe for all religions.

To be sure, "In the beginning God created the heavens and the earth," is a statement most Jews, Christians, or Muslims would agree with. However, John's telling of the creation story creates a conflict. He makes it all about Jesus: "God created everything through [Jesus], and nothing was created except through him" (1:3).

And the writer of Hebrews agrees when he writes, ". . . through the Son [God] made the universe and everything in it" (1:2 NLT 1996).

The author Sally Lloyd-Jones says it poetically in her children's book, *The Jesus Storybook Bible*, with the story of Jesus calming the storm over the Sea of Galilee: "The wind and the waves recognized Jesus' voice. (They had heard it before, of course—it was the same voice that made them, in the very beginning.)"[3]

In other words, before time . . . before creation . . . before sin . . . there was Jesus. The apostle Paul echoes John:

> Christ is the visible image of the invisible God.
>
> > He existed before anything was created and is supreme over all creation,
>
> for through him God created everything
>
> > in the heavenly realms and on earth.

---

3. Sally Lloyd-Jones, *The Jesus Storybook Bible: Every Story Whispers His Name* (Grand Rapids: Zonderkidz, 2012), 242.

> He made the things we can see
>> and the things we can't see—
> such as thrones, kingdoms, rulers, and authorities in
> the unseen world.
>> Everything was created through him and for him.
> He existed before anything else,
>> and he holds all creation together. (Col. 1:15–17)

Jesus is the one who created all of this. Jesus is the one who came down to be like one of us and redeem all this. And Jesus is the one who will come back and fully restore all of this.

In the beginning, Jesus. In the end, Jesus. It's why Advent is a season, not just a day.

Because seasons form us. They tell which stories have the power to control the trajectory of our desires, time, money, resources, and affections. We orient ourselves to seasons and, in turn, they orient us.

Think about it: football season; hunting season; the school calendar; the fiscal year; the sacred days like the Fourth of July and Super Bowl Sunday; these and others dominate the orbit of our lives.

It's why the seasons of the church calendar orbit around the life of Christ:

Advent: the return of Jesus to the world in final victory, because of . . .

Christmas: the birth of Jesus into the world, which leads to . . .

Epiphany: the manifestation of Jesus to the world, which leads to . . .

Lent: Jesus' journey to the cross for the world, which leads to . . .

Easter: the resurrection of Jesus in the world, which leads to . . .

Ascension: the enthronement of Jesus over the world, which leads to . . .

Pentecost: Jesus sending his Spirit into the world, which leads to . . .

Kingdomtide: proclaiming the good news of Jesus to the world, which leads to . . .

Advent: the return of Jesus to the world in final victory.

Remember, Advent is an opportunity to once again let the church's seasons, not the world's, set the orbit of our lives . . . for the sake of the world God loves.

So it's settled. Jesus really is the reason for the season. All of them.

CHRIST WAS BORN. CHRIST HAS DIED. CHRIST IS RISEN. CHRIST WILL COME AGAIN!

Apocalyptic Anxiety 4

MATTHEW 24:6–8, 29–30 | And you will hear of wars and threats of wars, but don't panic. Yes, these things must take place, but the end won't follow immediately. Nation will go to war against nation, and kingdom against kingdom. There will be famines and earthquakes in many parts of the world. But all this is only the first of the birth pains, with more to come. . . .

"Immediately after the anguish of those days,
the sun will be darkened,
the moon will give no light,
the stars will fall from the sky,
and the powers in the heavens will be shaken.

And then at last, the sign that the Son of Man is coming will appear in the heavens, and there will be deep mourning among all the peoples of the earth. And they will see the Son of Man coming on the clouds of heaven with power and great glory."

Consider This

We read Scripture like this and we panic.

The return of Jesus is the end of the world as we know it, and it sounds terrifying. Many of us go to extremes: we either avoid it or try to control it. We steer clear of preaching and teaching about it altogether or spend an unhealthy amount of time trying to figure out a road map of the end times.

That's what fear does, and as Jedi Master Yoda says, "Fear leads to anger, anger leads to hate, and hate leads to suffering."[4]

But Jesus says, "Don't panic. I'm coming in great glory."

So if his return is something to celebrate at Advent, why are

---

4. *Star Wars Episode I The Phantom Menace*, dir. by George Lucas (1999; 20th Century Fox, 2007 DVD).

we so afraid of it? Maybe before we look at what the return of Jesus is, we should look at what it isn't.

Here's a little story for you.

In my church youth group days, we spent a lot of time talking about how the world would end and getting married. For most us, the main takeaway was hoping we got married before Jesus came back.

But a lot of folks took it very seriously, including my mom's Sunday school teacher. Almost every lesson involved reading the headlines and getting ready for the end, which could come at any moment. She taught the class from cassette tapes and books by popular end-times preachers, who combined current events and Scripture in an attempt to predict a target date for the return of Christ. They said there would be global cataclysms to signal the end of the world, and the big question was, "Are you ready?"

Then one day, the teacher and her family disappeared. They sold their house, quit their jobs, and moved to rural Texas. They bought some remote property, stocked up on food, water, and other supplies . . . and waited.

And waited.

Five years later we saw them at the grocery store after they moved back.

Don't panic. I'm coming in great glory.

But panic has helped create an end-times industrial complex: preachers, teachers, conferences, books, movies— all aimed at predicting when Christ will return and what will happen to the world—have steadily flooded the Christian consumer market.

We're not the first to have this problem. Paul also dealt with it and gives a warning:

> "Don't be so easily shaken or alarmed by those who say that the day of the Lord has already begun. Don't believe them, even if they claim to have had a spiritual vision, a revelation, or a letter supposedly from us. Don't be fooled by what they say." (2 Thess. 2:2–3)

But people are still fooled, and at the heart of this complex is a theology that says an already dark world will be plunged into utter despair, Christians will be taken away, and Jesus will return to settle the score and wipe the whole place out.

This sounds more like revenge than restoration, and is that a reason to celebrate Advent? No.

The return of Jesus is part of the gospel, which is good news. Anything that operates out of fear and violence is not good news.

Don't panic. I'm coming in great glory.

Those wars, famines, and earthquakes—and the lives they destroy—aren't God's warm-up act for the end. They are the consequences of the sins Jesus is coming back to undo.

Whatever you believe about how the world will end in the future forms your posture to the world today. So things will be bad . . . and may get worse. But don't panic. He's going to come back in great glory. So let's stop spreading fear about it, and instead spread some joy to the world.

CHRIST WAS BORN. CHRIST HAS DIED. CHRIST IS RISEN. CHRIST WILL COME AGAIN!

Why Joy Is a Defiant Act 5

REVELATION 21:1–5 | Then I saw a new heaven and a new earth, for the old heaven and the old earth had disappeared. And the sea was also gone. And I saw the holy city, the new Jerusalem, coming down from God out of heaven like a bride beautifully dressed for her husband.

I heard a loud shout from the throne, saying, "Look, God's home is now among his people! He will live with them, and they will be his people. God himself will be with them. He will wipe every tear from their eyes, and there will be no more death or sorrow or crying or pain. All these things are gone forever."

And the one sitting on the throne said, "Look, I am making everything new!"

Consider This

The previous chapter ended with a call to spread joy, not fear, about the end of the world.

Joy? Yes . . . joy. Consider the song we sing as a Christmas carol, but is really an Advent anthem, "Joy to the World":

Joy to the world, the Lord is come!
Let earth receive her King;
Let every heart prepare him room,
And heaven and nature sing,
And heaven and nature sing,
And heaven, and heaven, and nature sing.

In this chapter, we see God's future mission completion to redeem our mission failure: a new heaven and a new earth, with no more of the sorrow and pain of this world. That's a reason to celebrate, right?

But what if there's more going on than God calling for a cosmic do-over and replacing this world with a new one?

The late great Robert Mulholland wrote that the Greek word translated "new" here is *kinos*, which implies *renewed*, not brand new . . . a change in quality or essence, rather than something that never existed before.[5]

In other words, maybe Jesus is not returning to wipe this world out in fire and violence, but instead to restore *shalom*. We translate that word "peace," but this kind of peace is more than just the absence of conflict. It is understood as wholeness and well-being, the gift from God that was lost in Eden and recovered by the Prince of Peace.[6]

> Joy to the world, the Savior reigns!
> Let men their songs employ;
> While fields and floods, rocks, hills, and plains
> Repeat the sounding joy,
> Repeat the sounding joy,
> Repeat, repeat, the sounding joy.

N. T. Wright says, "if God really does intend to *redeem* rather than reject his created world . . . we are faced with the

---

5. M. Robert Mulholland, *Revelation: Holy Living in an Unholy World* (Grand Rapids: Francis Asbury Press, 1990), 315.
6. Paul J. Achtemeier, general editor, *The HarperCollins Bible Dictionary* (San Francisco: HarperCollins, 1996).

question: what might it look like to celebrate that redemption, that healing and transformation, in the present, and thereby appropriately anticipate God's final intention?"[7]

If the gospel of Jesus Christ isn't good news for the future, then it isn't good news for the present. Advent is about hearing the story from the future and allowing it to speak joy into the darkest places *now*.

And it can't just be good news for me in my comfy, middle-class American life. The future has to be good news wherever there is darkness in the world. Advent is saying this world is not how it was supposed to be, and it's not how it's going to be.

Is the future good news for the city of Aleppo? For the daughter sitting next to her dying mother in hospice? For refugees forced from their homes and land? For the teenage girl trapped as a sex slave? For the lands decimated by consumption? For the father with depression trying every medication? For race relations? For the gunshot victim? For the pastor with a porn addiction?

> No more let sins and sorrows grow,
> nor thorns infest the ground;
> He comes to make his blessings flow
> Far as the curse is found,
> Far as the curse is found,
> Far as, far as, the curse is found.

---

7. N. T. Wright, *Surprised by Hope: Rethinking Heaven, the Resurrection, and the Mission of the Church* (New York: Harper One, 2008), 212.

I once heard U2's Bono say that joy is a defiant act against our mortality.[8] Let all the people say amen because this future is good news against the curse that brought death to us all. We can have joy in the middle of tragedy and darkness today because of what Advent is saying about tomorrow.

> He rules the world with truth and grace
> And makes the nations prove
> The glories of his righteousness,
> And wonders of his love,
> And wonders of his love,
> And wonders, wonders, of his love.[9]

CHRIST WAS BORN. CHRIST HAS DIED. CHRIST IS RISEN. CHRIST WILL COME AGAIN!

6 Anticipating the Verdict

PSALM 96:11–13 | Let the heavens be glad, and the earth rejoice!

Let the sea and everything in it shout his praise!
Let the fields and their crops burst out with joy!
Let the trees of the forest sing for joy

---

8. "Bono Explains the Emotional Landscapes of 'Songs of Experience,'" interview with Bill Flanagan on "Written in My Soul," October 18, 2017, www.soundcloud .com/siriusxmentertainment/bono-explains-the-emotional-landscapes-of-songs -of-experience.

9. Isaac Watts, "Joy to the World," Public Domain.

before the Lord, for he is coming!
  He is coming to judge the earth.
He will judge the world with justice,
  and the nations with his truth.

Consider This

Last chapter we looked at how the return of Jesus is good news that should bring joy, not fear. But another reason we may not be ready for his return (or want it to happen) is because of one little word that comes back with Christ: judgment.

I've been called for jury duty once. It was a civil case involving a hospital. Someone had done something wrong, and someone had to pay . . . a lot. I was the last potential juror sent home. When the judge called my number and said I could go, I was a little bummed. I wanted to see it play out. I had visions in my head from every courtroom drama I'd ever watched.

But honestly, I wanted to see someone get their come-uppance. Isn't anticipating the verdict the best part of a courtroom scene? Think of all the major court cases that have played out in real life in our country . . . millions waiting to hear if their version of justice will be handed down, and then many responding with either relief or rage.

We tend to think of a judge as someone who frees those who are innocent, but more often hands down punishment to those who have done wrong. And if we're honest, many times when we say "justice" what we really mean is "revenge."

But my friend Steve Seamands explains in his book *Give Them Christ* how in the days of the Bible, judgment was "not primarily about rewards and punishments or balancing scales, but about fixing what's been broken and making wrong things right."[10]

He points to N. T. Wright, who explains judgment as a *celebration* of today's text: "In a world of systematic injustice, bullying, violence, arrogance, and oppression, the thought that there might come a day when the wicked are firmly put in their place and the poor and weak are given their due is the best news there can be."[11]

There's that idea again: Jesus coming back as good news.

So what verdict are we anticipating from Christ when he returns? What will his judgment be? Let the psalmist give us a clue:

> But joyful are those who have the God of Israel as their
>   helper,
>   whose hope is in the LORD their God.
> He made heaven and earth,
>   the sea, and everything in them.
>   He keeps every promise forever.
> He gives justice to the oppressed
>   and food to the hungry.
> The LORD frees the prisoners.
>   The LORD opens the eyes of the blind.

---

10. Seamands, *Give Them Christ*, 172.
11. Wright, *Surprised by Hope*, 137.

The LORD lifts up those who are weighed down.
> The LORD loves the godly.
The LORD protects the foreigners among us.
> He cares for the orphans and widows,
> but he frustrates the plans of the wicked. (Ps. 146:5–9)

What do we want? Justice.
When do we want it? Now.
Come quickly, Lord Jesus!

CHRIST WAS BORN. CHRIST HAS DIED. CHRIST IS RISEN. CHRIST WILL COME AGAIN!

What Have You Been Doing All This Time?

7

MATTHEW 24:36–44 | "However, no one knows the day or hour when these things will happen, not even the angels in heaven or the Son himself. Only the Father knows.

"When the Son of Man returns, it will be like it was in Noah's day. In those days before the flood, the people were enjoying banquets and parties and weddings right up to the time Noah entered his boat. People didn't realize what was going to happen until the flood came and swept them all away. That is the way it will be when the Son of Man comes.

"Two men will be working together in the field; one will be taken, the other left. Two women will be grinding flour at the mill; one will be taken, the other left.

"So you, too, must keep watch! For you don't know what day your Lord is coming. Understand this: If a homeowner knew exactly when a burglar was coming, he would keep watch and not permit his house to be broken into. You also must be ready all the time, for the Son of Man will come when least expected."

Consider This

For twenty-six years my father traveled from Dallas, Texas, to Cairo, Egypt, for work. He was usually gone between three and six months, but sometimes it was longer.

Dad runs a tight ship, but the second the wheels on his plane went up, my mom, little brother, and I would immediately put things to our liking. No eating in the living room? Not anymore. The dog isn't allowed in the house? Guess who's cuddled up on the sofa taking a nap. Finish my homework first? My favorite show is on, so I'll watch it while eating pancakes for dinner in the living room while feeding bacon to the dog.

We slacked off on everything . . . until the phone call. The one saying he was in the air and would be home in a few hours.

We never knew when he would return. We always thought we'd know well in advance and have time to get things in order. There would be rumors, and plans would be made, but there was always something to hold him up. So it became common practice for his office to wait until he was on a plane, somewhere over the Atlantic, before they would let us know.

So we panicked. Now it was all hands on deck! Vacuum the dog dander off the cushions! Throw something that wasn't pancakes, pizza, or takeout in the oven for dinner! Is the dog still in the house?

We made big "Welcome Home, Dad!" banners and hung them from the fireplace mantle. There would be hugs and gifts, unpacking of bags, a big family dinner, and then a night's sleep to overcome the jet lag.

Then my father would wake up and get to work. He would pore over every statement, bill, and report card piled up in his absence . . . then lay out the evidence of money that shouldn't have been spent, late payments on bills, slipping grades, dog hairs on the carpet, and no real food in the pantry.

Then came his judgment. "What have you been doing while I was gone? I expect you to be the same person while I'm away that you are when I'm here."

Previously, we saw that when Jesus returns, his judgment for the world will primarily be about fixing what is broken and restoring what was lost.

But what about his judgment for us who are believers? Do we have a role to play *now*, before his arrival, where he'll hold us to account?

We think we've got enough time, but we get distracted by our own wants (and sometimes by trying to figure out when he'll return) instead of who we'll be and what we'll be doing when he does return. Jesus gives us believers a pretty clear expectation of what he'll judge us for while he's away.

First, the arrival:

> "But when the Son of Man comes in his glory, and all the angels with him, then he will sit upon his glorious throne. All the nations will be gathered in his presence, and he will separate the people as a shepherd separates the sheep from the goats. He will place the sheep at his right hand and the goats at his left." (Matt. 25:31–33)

Then, the expectation:

> "Then the King will say to those on his right, 'Come, you who are blessed by my Father, inherit the Kingdom prepared for you from the creation of the world. For I was hungry, and you fed me. I was thirsty, and you gave me a drink. I was a stranger, and you invited me into your home. I was naked, and you gave me clothing. I was sick, and you cared for me. I was in prison, and you visited me.'" (Matt. 25:34–36)

And, finally, the criteria:

> "when you did it to one of the least of these my brothers and sisters, you were doing it to me!" (Matt. 25:40)

So how do we get ready so we don't have to scramble when we get the call he's coming back?

CHRIST WAS BORN. CHRIST HAS DIED. CHRIST IS RISEN. CHRIST WILL COME AGAIN!

Wedding Rehearsing or Wedding Crashing?

8

MATTHEW 25:1–13 | "Then the Kingdom of Heaven will be like ten bridesmaids who took their lamps and went to meet the bridegroom. Five of them were foolish, and five were wise. The five who were foolish didn't take enough olive oil for their lamps, but the other five were wise enough to take along extra oil. When the bridegroom was delayed, they all became drowsy and fell asleep.

"At midnight they were roused by the shout, 'Look, the bridegroom is coming! Come out and meet him!'

"All the bridesmaids got up and prepared their lamps. Then the five foolish ones asked the others, 'Please give us some of your oil because our lamps are going out.'

"But the others replied, 'We don't have enough for all of us. Go to a shop and buy some for yourselves.'

"But while they were gone to buy oil, the bridegroom came. Then those who were ready went in with him to the marriage feast, and the door was locked. Later, when the other five bridesmaids returned, they stood outside, calling, 'Lord! Lord! Open the door for us!'

"But he called back, 'Believe me, I don't know you!'

"So you, too, must keep watch! For you do not know the day or hour of my return."

Consider This

I've officiated dozens of weddings, and almost all of them share a common practice: the wedding rehearsal. Everyone gathers the night before the ceremony to do a run-through. Everyone practices when they will walk in, where they will stand, how the ceremony will flow, and how they'll process out. The rehearsal makes sure that when the real wedding arrives, everyone is prepared.

Weddings play a big part in the salvation story. This whole thing started with a wedding in a garden that didn't end well. Jesus performed his first miracle at a wedding, turning water into wine as a sign of what was to happen on the cross.

And then there is this very Advent line Jesus drops to his disciples:

> My Father's house has many rooms; if that were not so, would I have told you that I am going there to prepare a place for you? And if I go and prepare a place for you, I will come back and take you to be with me that you also may be where I am. (John 14:2–3 NIV)

This is wedding language. In the ancient Middle East, after a couple was engaged, the custom was for the groom to return to his father's home, which was known as the "four-bedroom house." There, his father and he would build another four-bedroom house attached to the father's. There would be add-ons and add-ons until two to three generations of families were living around the father's house.

When it was time for the wedding, the groom and his entourage would proceed to the bride's home, and together they would return to the father's house, get married, celebrate with a big wedding feast in the father's dining room, then party for days.

This is where today's text comes in. The bridesmaids don't know when the groom is coming back for the procession to the father's house. And we see with the oil lamps that all of them were waiting in anticipation for his return *to* happen, but only half were prepared for *when* it might happen.

The bridesmaids who had extra oil in their lamps had prepared and were ready, even though they fell asleep. The ones who woke up with nothing were waiting and anticipating the wedding would happen at any moment, but got caught unprepared.

Then they foolishly depended on the resources of the others who were ready. It's as if their pre-wedding posture was, "I don't need enough oil because I'm with people who already have enough. I'm good if I hang out with them."

And know this: Jesus' story is an in-house critique. He's not talking about the lost here; he's warning those who have answered the question, "If you died tonight, do you know where you'd spend eternity?"

Many of us are like the foolish bridesmaids: instead of owning our role in getting prepared, we outsource our readiness, as if simply being associated with the right people at the right time will get us in. As one good friend said, we want Jesus to come back and rescue us, and we've got our confirmation class certificate, tithe statement, and recipes from the church potluck ready to show and say, "I'm ready!"

There's an urgent difference between *anticipating* and *preparing*; between *waiting* and being *ready* for Jesus to return.

Like any good wedding ceremony, there's a rehearsal. We get prepared by rehearsing now what it will be like when we're in his father's house. That rehearsal starts with the meal when we gather in worship and celebrate the Lord's Supper . . . the one Jesus said he wouldn't eat with us until he returned and we eat it together in his father's kingdom.

This meal is the heart of our Advent mission, and at the heart of the meal is a prayer. And at the heart of the prayer, we pray that the bread and wine would "become for us the body and blood of Jesus Christ, that we might be for the world the body of Christ redeemed by his blood."

This meal prepares us for our Advent mission, as we wait to hear the angels say:

> "The time has come for the wedding feast of the Lamb,
>   and his bride has prepared herself.
> She has been given the finest of pure white linen to wear."
>   For the fine linen represents the good deeds of God's holy people.
>
> And the angel said to me, "Write this: Blessed are those who are invited to the wedding feast of the Lamb."
> (Rev. 19:7–9)

CHRIST WAS BORN. CHRIST HAS DIED. CHRIST IS RISEN. CHRIST WILL COME AGAIN!

Why Waiting Is Active

9

ISAIAH 35:1–6 | Even the wilderness and desert will be glad
in those days.

The wasteland will rejoice and blossom with spring
crocuses.
Yes, there will be an abundance of flowers
and singing and joy!
The deserts will become as green as the mountains of
Lebanon,
as lovely as Mount Carmel or the plain of Sharon.
There the Lord will display his glory,
the splendor of our God.
With this news, strengthen those who have tired hands,
and encourage those who have weak knees.
Say to those with fearful hearts,
"Be strong, and do not fear,
for your God is coming to destroy your enemies.
He is coming to save you."

And when he comes, he will open the eyes of the blind
and unplug the ears of the deaf.
The lame will leap like a deer,
and those who cannot speak will sing for joy!
Springs will gush forth in the wilderness,
and streams will water the wasteland.

Consider This

In this text, the prophet Isaiah tells the story of a people freed from their slavery to the consequences of sin. Looking to the future, he says the rescue of humanity, and the restoration of God's kingdom, would be when the eyes of the blind were opened, the ears of the deaf were unstopped, and the lame leaped like deer.

In the New Testament, when John the Baptist was in prison, he sent a message to Jesus and asked if he was the Rescuer (see Matthew 11:2–3). Was he bringing the kingdom, or would it be someone else? What's interesting is that Jesus doesn't just answer yes or no, he responds by subversive code:

> John the Baptist, who was in prison, heard about all the things the Messiah was doing. So he sent his disciples to ask Jesus, "Are you the Messiah we've been expecting, or should we keep looking for someone else?"
>
> Jesus told them, "Go back to John and tell him what you have heard and seen—the blind see, the lame walk, those with leprosy are cured, the deaf hear, the dead are raised to life, and the Good News is being preached to the poor." (Matt. 11:2–5)

There's a tension here called the "already/not yet." Jesus is on the scene to establish his kingdom by his life, death, resurrection, and ascension. But it will not be fully realized until he returns. We call this the "already/not yet" because his kingdom is already here, but it has not yet had final victory.

We're waiting for Jesus to return, and waiting is active. Into this tension Advent gives us our mission.

To illustrate what this looks like consider the story of the Underground Railroad: The secret network of individuals, groups, churches, and others who helped slaves escape from the South to the North and Canada.

Though Abraham Lincoln had *not yet* delivered the Emancipation Proclamation, the people of the Underground Railroad lived as though it had *already* happened, and so worked to free as many slaves as they could, usually by subversive means.[12]

One such story of subversion is the tale of Dr. Alexander Ross. After a conversation with an abolitionist, a convicted Dr. Ross became creative in helping slaves escape by pretending to be a scientist studying birds. This ruse would allow him onto plantations, where he would quietly give slaves information on routes of escape. Sometimes he would offer them food, money, compasses, weapons, and the names of people who would shelter them.

He once pretended a female slave was his personal servant and led her all the way to Ontario to be reunited with her

---

12. Howard Snyder, "Waiting in Eager Expectation," Asbury Theological Seminary, Wilmore, KY, October 18, 2005.

husband. According to his records, Ross helped free at least thirty-one slaves.[13]

Subversion. It means "the undermining of the power and authority of an established system or institution."

This is how we get ready for his return, to go subversively among the plantations of sin and take the time to walk with that one person to freedom. To live our lives in the upside down of the already/not yet—helping the blind see, the deaf hear, and the lame walk—as we wait in hope for Christ our Judge to return and proclaim a final emancipation from the world's slavery to sin and death.

CHRIST WAS BORN. CHRIST HAS DIED. CHRIST IS RISEN. CHRIST WILL COME AGAIN!

10 Why Advent Is More than Social Justice Awareness

EPHESIANS 1:7–10 | He is so rich in kindness and grace that he purchased our freedom with the blood of his Son and forgave our sins. He has showered his kindness on us, along with all wisdom and understanding.

---

13. Information plaque, "Alexander Ross: Rescuing 'Flocks' of Runaways," Cincinnati, OH: National Underground Railroad Freedom Center, 2010.

God has now revealed to us his mysterious will regarding Christ—which is to fulfill his own good plan. And this is the plan: At the right time he will bring everything together under the authority of Christ—everything in heaven and on earth.

Consider This

The last couple of chapters we've looked at our Advent mission as acts of social justice in the world. But this is a good time to pause and look carefully at our trajectory. Today's text reminds us that the final mission plan is not only works of justice, but for everything in heaven and earth to be brought together in Christ.

Early in Advent we looked at how Jesus is the One who created all of this so of course his final mission will be to bring it all together in himself. In other words, Advent is more than social justice awareness month.

The truth is we don't need a gospel message for social justice. Even the pagans are for that. I've been a part of several interfaith services, and the one thing they all have in common is prayers for peace and calls for justice.

Don't get me wrong . . . it's a good thing, but what does it really mean? Does peace mean the absence of conflict? No more war? No more political Twitter trolling? Partially . . . but in Scripture peace means so much more than that.

Remember, the word is *shalom*, and it means wholeness and well-being—the ideal state of humanity, both individual and communal—as a gift from God. It's what we had and lost in Eden, and Advent reminds us that it's only found again in Jesus Christ. As Paul says:

> For God in all his fullness
>> was pleased to live in Christ,
> and through him God reconciled
>> everything to himself.
> He made peace with everything in heaven and on earth
>> by means of Christ's blood on the cross. (Col. 1:19–20)

Advent aims to deepen our mission understanding of "for God so loved the world that he sent his only Son," and widen our orbit beyond only social justice.

As Andy Crouch writes:

> Attempt to bring justice without Jesus, and you may not even get justice. You will certainly not get justice the way the Bible understands it—the restoration of all things to their created fruitfulness with the One who made them. . . . If you follow Jesus, he will use you to bring justice. If you want justice—follow Jesus.[14]

Because what we're aiming for is,

> "After this I saw a vast crowd, too great to count, from every nation and tribe and people and language, standing in front of the throne and before the Lamb. They were clothed in white robes and held palm branches in their hands. And they were shouting with

---

14. Andy Crouch, "No Jesus, No Justice," January 9, 2014, http://andy-crouch. com/articles/no_jesus_no_justice.

a great roar, 'Salvation comes from our God who sits on the throne and from the Lamb!'" (Rev. 7:9–10)

So next we should probably talk about how to get into mission mode.

CHRIST WAS BORN. CHRIST HAS DIED. CHRIST IS RISEN. CHRIST WILL COME AGAIN!

Stopping for Directions 11

MATTHEW 3:1–3 | In those days John the Baptist came to the Judean wilderness and began preaching. His message was, "Repent of your sins and turn to God, for the Kingdom of Heaven is near."

The prophet Isaiah was speaking about John when he said,
"He is a voice shouting in the wilderness,
'Prepare the way for the Lord's coming!
Clear the road for him!'"

Consider This

We're halfway through our Advent mission, so let's take a look at our trajectory so far. We remember that Advent breaks into our present darkness with hope from the future, where Jesus will come back to remake the world he created. Until he comes back, we are to live as though it's already happened, bringing the good news to everyone.

Sounds simple enough. So then why aren't we there yet?

I think it's more mission failure. We mean well, and we want to follow Jesus in his mission now. But our sins, brokenness, and distractions keep pushing us off course, leaving us wondering where we're going.

So what do we do? We begin where the prophet John did when he announced Jesus' mission with repentance: *Repent of your sins and turn to God, for the Kingdom of Heaven is near.*

Remember, Advent is a season to help us reorient our lives to Jesus, and repentance is where we start. The problem is, many of us have a distorted definition of repentance. We tend to think of it as feeling guilty for what we've done, promising not to do it again, and then working hard at behavior management to keep that promise.

We look at repentance as walking *away* from something, but actually repentance is reorienting us *to* something. In this case, someone.

John's idea of repentance would have been formed by its Hebrew word *shub*, which means, "To turn back and retrace your steps, in order to return by the right way."[15]

Here's what that looks like: I have no sense of direction. None. Zero. Even when the sun is setting, I get confused which way is west. I get lost in my own house. It's even worse on the road, especially if I have to go to a new part of town. "It's just a couple of minutes north of the mall," my wife will say.

---

15. Achtemeier, ed., *The HarperCollins Bible Dictionary*.

Okay. I've been to the mall . . . I can do that. I pass the mall . . . it's been two minutes. Or was it two miles? Now it's been five minutes. Now seven. Now I'm in another town.

Turn around. Go back by the right path.

Wait—that McDonald's looks familiar. I think I should have turned there. Make another turn. Two minutes. Four. Six. Not it.

Turn around. Go back by the right path.

Once, when driving from Dallas to Tulsa, I made a pit stop halfway through the trip. I got back on the highway and drove for another hour. As I crossed the state line back into Texas, I realized I had turned south instead of north.

Yep . . . one hour in the wrong direction. Turn around. Go back by the right path.

Before the iPhone, I would have stopped at a gas station for directions after the third or fourth U-turn. Now I pull over and try to figure out where the little blue dot on Google Maps says I am. But sometimes I go a while before I realize I'm not where I was intended to be.

I asked my wife how she always knows which way we're going, can find a new way to get there, and still never get lost. "Easy," she said, "I just remember which way is north, and then I can tell which roads will go what direction to get me there."

"I wish I could do that," I said. She pointed at the little digital compass mounted in my rearview mirror and said I can always start there to reorient myself.

This is why we take a *season*, not just a day, to prepare for Christ's return. Because repentance is not about working up more guilt or a redoubling of sin management efforts. Repentance is remembering and reorienting ourselves to the right path, which is Jesus . . . who is the way, the truth, and the life. It's a constant stopping and turning around on the highway of holiness.

But we can't do it alone.

CHRIST WAS BORN. CHRIST HAS DIED. CHRIST IS RISEN. CHRIST WILL COME AGAIN!

12 | Course Correction

HEBREWS 10:23–25 | Let us hold tightly without wavering to the hope we affirm, for God can be trusted to keep his promise. Let us think of ways to motivate one another to acts of love and good works. And let us not neglect our meeting together, as some people do, but encourage one another, especially now that the day of his return is drawing near.

Consider This

We defined repentance as reorienting to the right path. If Advent is the season where we can reorient ourselves to Jesus and his final mission for the world, then what does that repentance look like?

Remember the story of Apollo 13, the spacecraft carrying three astronauts to the moon when an oxygen tank exploded? Their mission immediately changed. They were no longer going to land on the moon. Their new mission was to stay alive and get back to Earth.

But were they even going the right way? To navigate their way home, the crew needed to locate certain stars and constellations. But when they looked out the window, they saw thousands of false stars created by debris from the explosion. They couldn't tell the real stars from the fake ones.

They had to reorient using the sun, and it took all three of them to do it. One on the navigation controls, one checking the crosshairs on the telescope, and one looking out the window to call out when the sun came around.

But then their trajectory kept shifting off course. If they were just a tiny degree off course now, they'd miss the Earth completely by 200,000 miles. Each minute they were getting closer to Earth, and so they needed an immediate course correction. And again, it would take all three of them to do it. One timing how long to burn the engines, one steering the ship left and right, and one steering it up and down.[16]

This wasn't how they were supposed to fly their spaceship, but it worked.

What does all this have to do with repentance? The trajectory of our sin may seem small now, but down the road it can have devastating consequences. Repentance is about course

---

16. Jim Lovell and Jeffrey Kluger, *Lost Moon: The Perilous Voyage of Apollo 13* (New York: Houghton Mifflin Company, 1994).

correction. It is less about what we're moving away from and more about Who we're moving toward.

And the key to course correction is that we can't do it alone: "Confess your sins to each other and pray for each other so that you may be healed. The earnest prayer of a righteous person has great power and produces wonderful results" (James 5:16).

> Two people are better off than one, for they can help each other succeed. If one person falls, the other can reach out and help. But someone who falls alone is in real trouble. Likewise, two people lying close together can keep each other warm. But how can one be warm alone? A person standing alone can be attacked and defeated, but two can stand back-to-back and conquer. Three are even better, for a triple-braided cord is not easily broken. (Ecc. 4:9–12)

I'm in what John Wesley called a discipleship band with two other guys. At Seedbed we define a *discipleship band* as three to five people who read together, pray together, and meet together to become the love of God for one another and the world.

Even though we live in different states, we conference call every week and share the state of our soul, what possibilities there are in our lives for transformation, and what's in the way. We confess sins, admit temptations, grieve with each other, celebrate with each other, and speak into each other's lives.[17]

---

17. To learn more about discipleship bands and how to get into one, check out www.discipleshipbands.

Our trajectories keep going off course away from Christ. So like the three astronauts side by side in the Apollo capsule, we call out to each other. We help each other see what the other can't as we navigate through the fake lights of this world, pointing each other's trajectory back toward Christ. They are my mission crewmates.

That's what real repentance looks like. Remember, Advent is about the final stage of God's new mission that resulted from our mission failure. Repentance as course correction is how we get on board.

But trajectory and course correction are only part of the story. There was something else needed to get our astronauts home, and it's something we need, too.

CHRIST WAS BORN. CHRIST HAS DIED. CHRIST IS RISEN. CHRIST WILL COME AGAIN!

Why We Need to Shut Down

13

MATTHEW 6:31–34 | "So don't worry about these things, saying, 'What will we eat? What will we drink? What will we wear?' These things dominate the thoughts of unbelievers, but your heavenly Father already knows all your needs. Seek the Kingdom of God above all else, and live righteously, and he will give you everything you need.

"So don't worry about tomorrow, for tomorrow will bring its own worries. Today's trouble is enough for today."

Consider This

Let's stay with the crew of Apollo 13 and their mission to survive. We've looked at their story as an illustration of repentance as course correction. But we said there was something else needed to get them home that could shed some Advent light for us. What is it?

Shutting down.

When their oxygen tank exploded, it didn't just affect their trajectory, it also affected their systems. Their broken systems were draining too much power and threatening their life support.

In order to survive to reentry, the three astronauts would have to shut down the computer and electrical systems, then figure out how to resequence them to power back up. If they didn't, they would run out of power before they made it back to Earth.

What does all this have to do with Advent? Well, if Advent is a season of repentance, part of that process is looking at what systems are threatening our life support, and then shutting them down.

And I'd argue the system that most threatens our life support as believers is fear.

I've noticed that so many Christians are drained by fear. Some of the most fearful people I know are Christians. Not a prayer request session goes by without someone sharing a fear of what the world is coming to.

I'm not trying to minimize the fact that when we look at the news, there's a lot to cause anxiety, but aren't we the people Jesus explicitly told to not be afraid? Like with Eve in Eden and Jesus in the wilderness, the enemy plants seeds of doubt: "Did God really say that?" (see Genesis 3:1 and Matthew 4:1–11).

But the brokenness of fear drains our life support, threatening our very love and joy and peace and patience and gentleness. Fear drains us, causing us to either attack or self-medicate. This leaves us with anger at what's happening around us, hatred of people different than us, and ultimately the suffering of our lives and souls, and those of others.

Fear is a broken system that needs to be shut down and resequenced. What are the fear systems draining your life support, and how do they do it? For me, it can look like spending five minutes in prayer, but three hours in cable news, social media, and talk radio.

What would shutting that down and resequencing look like? And how would it affect the life support of my soul?

Advent is all about the mission, and the mission needs power. Maybe shutting down is really the way to power up. I'll let the psalmist have the last word today:

> Come, see the glorious works of the LORD:
>> See how he brings destruction upon the world.
> He causes wars to end throughout the earth.
>> He breaks the bow and snaps the spear;
>> he burns the shields with fire.

"Be still, and know that I am God!
  I will be honored by every nation.
  I will be honored throughout the world." (Ps. 46:8–10)

But as we'll see next, there's more to resequencing than shutting down.

CHRIST WAS BORN. CHRIST HAS DIED. CHRIST IS RISEN. CHRIST WILL COME AGAIN!

14 The Holiday ~~Feast~~ Fast

JOEL 2:12–15 NIV | "Even now," declares the LORD,
  "return to me with all your heart,
  with fasting and weeping and mourning."

Rend your heart
  and not your garments.
Return to the LORD your God,
  for he is gracious and compassionate,
slow to anger and abounding in love,
  and he relents from sending calamity.
Who knows? He may turn and relent
  and leave behind a blessing—
grain offerings and drink offerings
  for the LORD your God.

> Blow the trumpet in Zion,
>> declare a holy fast,
>> call a sacred assembly.

Consider This

We tend to think of fasting as something we do (if we do it) during Lent. But did you ever notice that the liturgical colors of both Lent and Advent are purple? That's because Advent traditionally was also a season for repentance (which we've talked about) *and* fasting.

But it's hard to find a rhythm of fasting when all we do is feast. Let's look at the story of my calendar, starting in a strange place: September.

School has just started back, football season is kicking off, and the Halloween costumes and candy are on the store shelves. The increased candy eating begins, weeks before the little ones come knocking on the door.

Then, on the first day of November, the Christmas candy and decorations invade everything. For the next couple of weeks, I'll keep eating Halloween candy, and then I'll take the third Thursday in November to eat my weight in turkey, sides, and pies. A few days later, just as the leftovers are finally drying up, the Christmas parties, baked goods, chocolate-covered cherries, and candy gift bags will begin to flow.

The eating continues long after the big present day, culminating with a New Year's Eve party and all its excess. By now, much of my diet has consisted of candy, cookies, and rich banquet foods for three solid months. So on that first January morning, I'm going to change everything: time to be a better person. Lose some weight. Live better.

Then the first sabotage. My birthday is in January. Cake. Fancy dinner. I'll restart after . . . the Super Bowl party the next week.

By now the Valentine's candy is on the shelves, and the girls are bringing home gift bags full of chocolate and candy, with all those heart-shaped boxes of chocolate beating for my affection from the checkout line.

And just when I think there's a break—even though the day after Valentine's the Cadbury Cream Eggs show up next to the register—it's all a setup. Like sirens, they call from outside the door to Walmart. They call and I cannot resist. Soon I am crashing into the rocks of Girl Scout cookies. Throw in an obligatory St. Patrick's Day green beer and all the Easter candy, and whatever goals I set in January are dead in the spring, even as the flowers are coming to life.

Memorial Day kicks off the cook-out season, with the Fourth of July being the biggest blast of them all. And so, by late summer, just as the tomatoes and cucumbers we planted in the backyard in the hopes of eating healthy and home-grown are fully ripening, the cycle is ready to start again. Back to school, and back to the Halloween candy on the shelves.

It makes sense that we are trapped in rabid consumption. After all, our mission failure began when someone ate some-thing. A moment of instant gratification that broke humanity and all of creation.

Jesus didn't say, "*if* you fast" but "*when* you fast" (see Matthew 6:16). We're called to it. But we don't fast to earn our salvation, prove our faithfulness, or manipulate God into answering our prayers. We fast to make a spiritual declaration that instant gratification will not control us, and to awaken us to our dependence on God.

Fasting during Advent is hard because everything around us this time of year is about eating more than ever. But Advent reorients us to God's rescue mission, which is grounded in self-giving instead of self-gratifying.

> No, the kind of fasting I want calls you to free those who are wrongly imprisoned and to stop oppressing those who work for you. Treat them fairly and give them what they earn. I want you to share your food with the hungry and to welcome the wanderers into your homes. Give clothes to those who need them, and do not hide from relatives who need your help. (Isa. 58:6–7 NLT 1996)

It's not easy to do in an all-you-can-eat culture. Fasting for a lot of us is like New Year's resolutions. We fail once and call it quits. So try fasting for one day a week . . . maybe just one meal during that one day and take the time you'd eat to pray and read Scripture. After all, people don't live by bread alone, but by every word that comes from the mouth of God.

One day Jesus will return, and we will all feast at his heavenly banquet table. Until then, let's prepare by calling a fast.

CHRIST WAS BORN. CHRIST HAS DIED. CHRIST IS RISEN. CHRIST WILL COME AGAIN!

15 The Final Countdown

2 PETER 3:3–4, 8–9 | Most importantly, I want to remind you that in the last days scoffers will come, mocking the truth and following their own desires. They will say, "What happened to the promise that Jesus is coming again?" . . .

But you must not forget this one thing, dear friends: A day is like a thousand years to the Lord, and a thousand years is like a day. The Lord isn't really being slow about his promise, as some people think. No, he is being patient for your sake. He does not want anyone to be destroyed, but wants everyone to repent.

Consider This

Did you ever make construction-paper Christmas countdown rings as a kid? Using alternating red and green strips, I'd staple them into interlocking rings, one for each day from December 1 until the lone yellow ring for Christmas Day. Each morning at breakfast I'd tear a ring off as our countdown clock: T-minus five days till presents!

And remember when the longest day of the year was? The day before Christmas, when there was only one green ring left. That day seemed to take forever. I remember once waking up at around 11:00 at night, believing the time had come and ran through the house literally ringing a bell to wake everyone to come open presents. My parents were not impressed. "It's not time yet!" they shouted me back to bed.

Dejected, I got under the covers and thought, *When is it ever going to happen?*

We've spent the last two weeks preparing for Jesus to return, each day tearing off another ring in preparation. But when is it ever going to happen? It's been about two thousand years, and the waiting is excruciating: "God, when are you sending Jesus? We're ready to be rescued here!"

But for God, it's only been a couple of days.

Let's pause and clear up one thing: "A day is like a thousand years to the Lord" is not a key to the secret math formula for predicting Jesus' return. It's a simile: a figure of speech where two unlike things are compared using *like* or *as* to make an emphatic description.

No one knows when it will be, not even Jesus (see Mark 13:32). Peter is saying that what seems like a long time to wait for us is not all that long to God. In fact, God is being patient.

Patience has always been God's way. After all, the entire Old Testament has God being patient. Think about how much time there was between Adam, Noah, Abraham, Moses, David, Isaiah . . . until John the Baptist announces the arrival of Jesus.

What's evident here is that God has more patience than we do because, "He does not want anyone to be destroyed, but wants everyone to repent" (v. 9).

His patience is *for* the sake of the lost. But did you catch who his patience is *with*? I didn't notice it either.

"No, he is being patient for your sake."

God is not being patient with them; he's being patient with us.

Why would God need to be patient for our sake if we already believe? Just come on and get us out of here, Lord!

God is being patient with us because we're the ones who are supposed to share the good news with those who would otherwise be destroyed. God has patience *for* the sake of the lost, but he is patient *with* us because we are the ones who are supposed to be calling them to repentance. In a sense, God's patience creates an urgency for us to share the good news before the final countdown.

This season of Advent is not just for us to prepare for Jesus' return; it is also a season where we, in the spirit of John the Baptist, call others to repentance . . . our lives like voices in the wilderness shouting:

> "Prepare the way for the Lord's coming!
>> Clear the road for him!
> The valleys will be filled,
>> and the mountains and hills made level.
> The curves will be straightened,
>> and the rough places made smooth.
> And then all people will see
>> the salvation sent from God." (Luke 3:4–6)[18]

---

18.   This connection between John the Baptist and us both "preparing the way of the Lord" came from Dorcas Beth Andrews in a discussion in the Daily Text Facebook group. You can join in the conversation at https://www.facebook.com/groups/thedailytext/.

Speaking of John the Baptist, here is where we make our pivot from the clouds to the cradle; from the end to the beginning, where our story will open on a waiting people asking, "God, when are you sending the Messiah? We're ready to be rescued here!"

Many had become impatient and so moved on. They were going about their business and had forgotten his promise. This means we're in good company. But as we're about to see, God always keeps his promises.

CHRIST WAS BORN. CHRIST HAS DIED. CHRIST IS RISEN. CHRIST WILL COME AGAIN!

Silent Nights (Part One) 16

LUKE 1:5–20 NLT 1996 | It all begins with a Jewish priest named Zechariah. He was a member of the priestly order of Abijah, and his wife, Elizabeth, was also from the priestly line of Aaron. Zechariah and Elizabeth were righteous in God's eyes, careful to obey all of the Lord's commandments and regulations. They had no children because Elizabeth was unable to conceive, and they were both very old.

One day Zechariah was serving God in the Temple, for his order was on duty that week. As was the custom of the priests, he was chosen by lot to enter the sanctuary of the Lord and burn incense. While the incense was being burned, a great crowd stood outside, praying.

While Zechariah was in the sanctuary, an angel of the Lord appeared to him, standing to the right of the incense altar. Zechariah was shaken and overwhelmed with fear when he saw him. But the angel said, "Don't be afraid, Zechariah! God has heard your prayer. Your wife, Elizabeth, will give you a son, and you are to name him John. You will have great joy and gladness, and many will rejoice at his birth, for he will be great in the eyes of the Lord. He must never touch wine or other alcoholic drinks. He will be filled with the Holy Spirit, even before his birth. And he will turn many Israelites to the Lord their God. He will be a man with the spirit and power of Elijah. He will prepare the people for the coming of the Lord. He will turn the hearts of the fathers to their children, and he will cause those who are rebellious to accept the wisdom of the godly."

Zechariah said to the angel, "How can I be sure this will happen? I'm an old man now, and my wife is also well along in years."

Then the angel said, "I am Gabriel! I stand in the very presence of God. It was he who sent me to bring you this good news! But now, since you didn't believe what I said, you will be silent and unable to speak until the child is born. For my words will certainly be fulfilled at the proper time."

Consider This

It all begins with a Jewish priest. It has the feel of *Once upon a time,* or *A long time ago, in a galaxy far, far away.* It sounds like a good start to a Christmas story, except that we never start here. Zechariah and Elizabeth never make the Christmas pageant. Their story is never in the children's picture book. They don't get a carol. No background appearance in the nativity scene.

When we go straight to Mary and skip this intro, we maybe miss something in the Advent turn from the clouds to the cradle. If the birth of Christ is the beginning of the new creation, then *It all begins* is Luke's "In the beginning" and it begins with a simple elderly temple priest and his wife, who had been unable to have children.

There's Zechariah, minding his own business, doing his priestly thing because it was his turn to keep the incense pot smoking. It was routine work that had been done for generations, but then something big happens that only he gets to see. The angel shows up and says, "God has heard your prayer. Your wife, Elizabeth, will give you a son" (v. 13).

And Zechariah doubted. We've seen this story before, with Abraham. He and Sarah were also elderly and childless, but God said he would create life where life couldn't happen in order to rescue humanity.

Abraham laughed. Zechariah didn't even get the chance to snicker: "since you didn't believe what I said, you will be silent and unable to speak until the child is born. For my words will certainly be fulfilled at the proper time" (v. 20).

We can think of doubt as being inconsequential, but for Zechariah it robbed him of something for nine months: the ability to tell everyone about the miracle God was doing.

The belief in Jerusalem was that at the proper time the prophet Elijah would return to prepare the way for the

Messiah. Everyone outside the temple was praying for Elijah to show up, but God was first inside answering one prayer in order to answer hundreds of thousands: "He will be a man with the spirit and power of Elijah, [to] prepare the people for the coming of the Lord" (v. 17).

And so when Zechariah came back outside, he couldn't talk.

These days, many folks enter the modern Christmas season with a sense of uncertainty in the world, and so want to be as big and loud and in your face about it as possible so everyone knows what we believe (think "war on Christmas" and "Merry Christmas vs. Happy Holidays").

But with God, it all begins with a silent night—actually nine months of them. So as we make the Advent turn together, let's find ways to be still and silent and know that he is God, because all this chatter could be festering doubt, distracting from the new thing that's beginning.

CHRIST WAS BORN. CHRIST HAS DIED. CHRIST IS RISEN. CHRIST WILL COME AGAIN!

17 Silent Nights (Part Two)

LUKE 1:57–64 | When it was time for Elizabeth's baby to be born, she gave birth to a son. And when her neighbors and relatives heard that the Lord had been very merciful to her, everyone rejoiced with her.

When the baby was eight days old, they all came for the circumcision ceremony. They wanted to name him Zechariah, after his father. But Elizabeth said, "No! His name is John!"

"What?" they exclaimed. "There is no one in all your family by that name." So they used gestures to ask the baby's father what he wanted to name him. He motioned for a writing tablet, and to everyone's surprise he wrote, "His name is John." Instantly Zechariah could speak again, and he began praising God.

Consider This

Names are a big deal in Middle Eastern culture, and keeping a family name is a big part of it. When our first daughter was born, all the Arab aunts, uncles, and cousins on my dad's side had suggestions. More importantly, in their Middle Eastern tribal culture, every child gets the father's first name as a middle name, even the girls. When we named her Sadie Renée (and Sadie is a Hebrew name) there was a collective, "Huh? What does that even mean?"

In today's story, all the aunts, uncles, and cousins would have been gathered for the circumcision ceremony. This was a big deal because it meant Zechariah and Elizabeth's son was entering the covenant. Of course, the miracle baby boy would have his father's name: Zech Jr. But God had a different name in mind, and when Elizabeth said, "No! His name is John!" (v. 60), their response was typical *My Big Fat Middle Eastern Family*: "What? . . . There is no one in all your family by that name" (v. 61). They didn't believe her until Zechariah scribbled it down because, remember, he couldn't talk. As we saw previously, the angel Gabriel gave him nine months of silent nights during the pregnancy because he wasn't ready to receive what he had been praying for.

But then he writes down the literal name to what God is doing—John—and suddenly he can speak again! And this time a very different voice comes out. Something happened in those nine silent months that moved Zechariah from crying a sigh of doubt to singing a hymn of faith:

"Praise the Lord, the God of Israel,
  because he has visited and redeemed his people.
He has sent us a mighty Savior
  from the royal line of his servant David,
just as he promised
  through his holy prophets long ago.
Now we will be saved from our enemies
  and from all who hate us.
He has been merciful to our ancestors
  by remembering his sacred covenant—
the covenant he swore with an oath
  to our ancestor Abraham.
We have been rescued from our enemies
  so we can serve God without fear,
in holiness and righteousness
  for as long as we live.

"And you, my little son,
  will be called the prophet of the Most High,
  because you will prepare the way for the Lord.

You will tell his people how to find salvation
through forgiveness of their sins.
Because of God's tender mercy,
the morning light from heaven is about to break
upon us,
to give light to those who sit in darkness and in the
shadow of death,
and to guide us to the path of peace." (Luke 1:68–79)

He may not keep the family name, but John will stay in the family business: preparing the way for the presence of the Lord.

Zechariah wasn't ready for what he had been praying for, but God gave him the grace of silence to prepare. Then, at the right time, Zechariah wrote John's name and not getting his daddy's name spoke something new into the world.

The people were looking for a messiah but, like Zechariah, they weren't ready for the answer to their prayers either. John's birth is a small answer to one prayer that will grow into a big answer to many prayers.

That's why Advent is a season to prepare for Christ's return *and* for his first arrival. Sometimes we need to be still and silent for a season so we can see where God is answering our prayers in unexpected ways, and then name them, so our lives can be an answer to many other prayers.

CHRIST WAS BORN. CHRIST HAS DIED. CHRIST IS RISEN. CHRIST WILL COME AGAIN!

18 | Why Mary Matters

LUKE 1:26–38 | In the sixth month of Elizabeth's pregnancy, God sent the angel Gabriel to Nazareth, a village in Galilee, to a virgin named Mary. She was engaged to be married to a man named Joseph, a descendant of King David. Gabriel appeared to her and said, "Greetings, favored woman! The Lord is with you!"

Confused and disturbed, Mary tried to think what the angel could mean. "Don't be afraid, Mary," the angel told her, "for you have found favor with God! You will conceive and give birth to a son, and you will name him Jesus. He will be very great and will be called the Son of the Most High. The Lord God will give him the throne of his ancestor David. And he will reign over Israel forever; his Kingdom will never end!"

Mary asked the angel, "But how can this happen? I am a virgin."

The angel replied, "The Holy Spirit will come upon you, and the power of the Most High will overshadow you. So the baby to be born will be holy, and he will be called the Son of God. What's more, your relative Elizabeth has become pregnant in her old age! People used to say she was barren, but she has conceived a son and is now in her sixth month. For the word of God will never fail."

Mary responded, "I am the Lord's servant. May everything you have said about me come true." And then the angel left her.

Consider This

One day when she was six years old, my oldest daughter said to me, "Daddy, when I grow up I want to be a boy." A little stunned, I asked her why. "Because," she said, "then I can be a preacher like you."

As best I could on a first-grade level, I explained to her a theology of why girls could be preachers too. In fact, I told her the first preacher in the Jesus story was a woman.

"Cool," she replied.

The first human to preach the good news in the New Testament was Mary. After the angel Gabriel delivers the news, she sings her first sermon:

> "Oh, how my soul praises the Lord.
>> How my spirit rejoices in God my Savior!
> For he took notice of his lowly servant girl,
>> and from now on all generations will call me blessed
> For the Mighty One is holy,
>> and he has done great things for me."
>
> (Luke 1:46–49)

Isn't it interesting that we don't look to Mary as a preacher or a disciple? We tend to look all year for discipleship cues from people like Moses, David, Peter, or Paul. But just once a year we look at Mary, and then usually reduce her and her womb to a utilitarian role.

I have a hunch part of the reason this happens is residual anti-Catholic bias. When I was growing up, I'd ask if someone else was a Christian, and the response could be, "No, she's a Catholic."

But in throwing the baby out with the holy water, we've missed seeing Mary as the first exemplar of discipleship: she is willing to lay down her life for Jesus. She is willing to give up her entitlements, all she's worked for, all she could be, and her reputation to have Jesus formed in her for the sake of the world.

Here comes the news that her life will be undone, and nothing will be the same again, and she replies with, "Oh how my soul praises the Lord." Later in her song she preaches:

> "He has helped his servant Israel
>   and remembered to be merciful.
> For he made this promise to our ancestors,
>   to Abraham and his children forever."
> (Luke 1:54–55)

Mary knows her God, and she knows the Scriptures. She is our first preacher and our first disciple, living her life where what she believes intersects with what she does.

Paul says in Colossians 1:27 that the mystery of God is, "Christ in you, the hope of glory" (NIV). Advent gives us another chance to embrace that mystery like Mary. To lay down our lives, entitlements, and reputations so the love of Christ can be formed in us, for the sake of the world.

May everything about this come true.

CHRIST WAS BORN. CHRIST HAS DIED. CHRIST IS RISEN. CHRIST WILL COME AGAIN!

The Dynamic Trio

19

LUKE 1:39–47 | A few days later Mary hurried to the hill country of Judea, to the town where Zechariah lived. She entered the house and greeted Elizabeth. At the sound of Mary's greeting, Elizabeth's child leaped within her, and Elizabeth was filled with the Holy Spirit.

Elizabeth gave a glad cry and exclaimed to Mary, "God has blessed you above all women, and your child is blessed. Why am I so honored, that the mother of my Lord should visit me? When I heard your greeting, the baby in my womb jumped for joy. You are blessed because you believed that the Lord would do what he said."

Mary responded,

"Oh, how my soul praises the Lord.
    How my spirit rejoices in God my Savior!"

Consider This

When my wife became pregnant with our first daughter, she immediately went out and bought the seminal parenting book *What to Expect When You're Expecting*. She saw doctors, took birthing classes, and nested in the bedroom. But most of all, she talked daily with her best friend, Allie, who already had three kids by this point. Those conversations were where real wisdom sharing, encouragement, and prayers happened.

Mary had none of this. No books. No doctors. No classes. And friends? She was a young girl pregnant out of wedlock, sure to be the shame of Nazareth once you could see her baby bump. Despite an angel delivering the good news of her miraculous pregnancy, Luke describes Mary as "confused and disturbed" (Luke 1:29). But the angel Gabriel mentioned her Aunt Elizabeth also being miraculously pregnant, so Mary bolted for her home in the hills.

Elizabeth had her own public humiliation to deal with. Women who couldn't have children endured public scorn, which is why when she found out she was pregnant she shouted, "How kind the Lord is! . . . He has taken away my disgrace of having no children" (Luke 1:25).

When she sees Mary, Aunt Elizabeth shouts with joy and becomes so filled with the Holy Spirit that her baby jumps in her belly. Now the three of them are there together: a young Mary, and old Elizabeth, and the Holy Spirit. Add the unborn John and Jesus, and there's five. My friend Carolyn Moore calls this the first New Testament discipleship band.

We looked at bands previously: A group of three to five people who read together, pray together, and meet together to become the love of God for one another and the world.

Carolyn says that when Elizabeth saw Mary, she did a very band thing:

> "She doesn't soothe Mary's emotional state. She speaks spiritually. She speaks prophetically over her, helping her to reinterpret her experience. 'You are blessed because you believed that the Lord would do what he said' (v. 45). Elizabeth speaks that word over a very confused young woman and the very next

sentence has Mary singing praise, like it all makes sense to her now."[19]

She goes on to say that the angel may have given Mary the news, but it was Elizabeth who made it *good news*, because the Holy Spirit gave power to bind their relationship together.

We are not intended to go through Advent—or any of our confusing and disturbing times—alone. We need others who help us see what we can't; to speak truth to our fears; to be the Aaron and Hur holding our arms up when we're under attack and grow tired (see Exodus 17:12).

Sometimes we're Elizabeth. Sometimes we're Mary. But both need the Holy Spirit, so that together the news, whatever it is, can become the good news.

CHRIST WAS BORN. CHRIST HAS DIED. CHRIST IS RISEN. CHRIST WILL COME AGAIN!

The Family Secret

20

JOHN 1:29–34 | The next day John saw Jesus coming toward him and said, "Look! The Lamb of God who takes away the sin of the world! He is the one I was talking about when I said, 'A man is coming after me who is far greater than I am, for he existed long before me.' I did not recognize him as the

---

19. Carolyn Moore, "Stay with It," presented at the New Room Conference, Fayetteville, Arkansas, March 15, 2018.

Messiah, but I have been baptizing with water so that he might be revealed to Israel."

Then John testified, "I saw the Holy Spirit descending like a dove from heaven and resting upon him. I didn't know he was the one, but when God sent me to baptize with water, he told me, 'The one on whom you see the Spirit descend and rest is the one who will baptize with the Holy Spirit.' I saw this happen to Jesus, so I testify that he is the Chosen One of God."

Consider This

The holiday season is often presented as a time of extended family celebration. I don't know what yours was like, but mine was not much to remember. My aunt, uncle, and two cousins would join us at my grandparents' farm for a couple of hours. We'd open presents, eat Christmas dinner, then it was hugs and, "See you again next year."

I always wanted a sort of "Christmas Cousins' Camp," but you can't build much of a relationship or series of memories on two hours a year. It wasn't until I was older and met the horde of my Arab cousins from my dad's side that the word "cousin" came to feel more like "blood brothers." From the moment we met, we were family and we were going to know everything about each other, call on each other, and defend each other.

This is the cultural world of John and Jesus. The first time these two cousins meet, the Holy Spirit stirs John in the water of the womb. The second time we see them together, the Holy Spirit settles on Jesus in the water of baptism.

So what about the thirty-year "cousin camp" in between? We saw how close their mothers were, so it's probably safe to assume they spent at least some time together growing up. I picture them playing together, fighting each other, getting into mischief during family feasts, and other typical growing-up-together things.

Maybe they were "cousin's camp" cousins or maybe they were "see you next year" cousins. Either way, they were blood family, so what does it mean that John had absolutely zero clue that his cousin was the Messiah?

They had to have spent time in Sabbath together, reading Scripture together, even talking about the prophecies of Isaiah they would quote back and forth later in the Gospels, right?

Even as John moved into his awkward "camel hair and locusts" prophet phase, telling everyone he was going to work to prepare for the coming of the Messiah, no one told him. Not. A. Clue.

Which can only lead to one possible conclusion: Mary never told anyone. Neither did Joseph, Elizabeth, or Zechariah. Jesus' true identity was the family secret until the right time, and then it was up to God for the big reveal.

It's the first time you hear Darth Vader say to Luke, "I am your father," and your jaw drops open with, "NO WAY" kind of big. Because there's John, who jumped with joy in utero over Jesus now jumping with joy on the shore, shouting, "I didn't know he was the one" (v. 33).

God promised John's father that his son would prepare the way of the Lord, and that's what John grew up preparing for.

But he had no clue that the Lord was as close as a cousin until the right moment.

There's an encouragement in this story for those who are alone or feel the Lord is far away, especially during the holidays. You've been praying and praying and praying, working and working and working . . . all the while believing, "At some point I'm going to see the Lord." That's the family secret of Advent: a whole season of expectation in our hearts and lives for the arrival of the Lord, who is always closer to us than we can think or imagine.

CHRIST WAS BORN. CHRIST HAS DIED. CHRIST IS RISEN. CHRIST WILL COME AGAIN!

21 The Scandal of the Manger

MATTHEW 1:18–25 | This is how Jesus the Messiah was born. His mother, Mary, was engaged to be married to Joseph. But before the marriage took place, while she was still a virgin, she became pregnant through the power of the Holy Spirit. Joseph, to whom she was engaged, was a righteous man and did not want to disgrace her publicly, so he decided to break the engagement quietly.

As he considered this, an angel of the Lord appeared to him in a dream. "Joseph, son of David," the angel said, "do not be afraid to take Mary as your wife. For the child within her was conceived by the Holy Spirit. And she will have a son, and you are to name him Jesus, for he will save his people from their sins."

All of this occurred to fulfill the Lord's message through his prophet:

> "Look! The virgin will conceive a child!
>   She will give birth to a son,
> and they will call him Immanuel,
>   which means 'God is with us.'"

When Joseph woke up, he did as the angel of the Lord commanded and took Mary as his wife. But he did not have sexual relations with her until her son was born. And Joseph named him Jesus.

Consider This

In high school, a girl I knew got pregnant, and she quietly left to what was then called a "home for unwed mothers." She stayed there until the child was born (who was quickly adopted) and then moved to another state.

It was quite the scandal. Everyone knew who she was with, and they *knew* who was responsible: her.

In today's text, when Mary turned out to be pregnant while still engaged to Joseph, it was going to be a scandal. So Joseph was ready to quietly leave.

Joseph's reputation, especially as a descendant of King David, was probably at stake. But in this patriarchal culture, the real victim of the scandal was Mary. In their culture, a couple who was engaged was considered legally married, they just hadn't consummated the marriage.

Under the law, if a woman became pregnant outside of this covenant, *she* was considered the adulterer, and the punishment was death by stoning. But as we saw previously, Mary was willing to lay down her life and endure a scandal to say yes to God's call.

We see God working through an unwed virgin, but take a closer look at the females Matthew includes in Jesus' genealogy, and we find a family of sex scandals. There's Tamar (pretended to be a prostitute and got pregnant by her father-in-law), Rahab (a prostitute), Ruth (slept with Boaz while he was passed out drunk), and Bathsheba (essentially raped by King David).

But where we see shame stories, God sees salvation stories.

Matthew's genealogy starts with Abraham (who had a little scandal of his own). But take an even closer look—all the way to the very beginning of the family tree—and we see an even greater scandal involving all of us.

In the very beginning, the Spirit hovers over the water of chaos, and God creates light and dark, oceans and sky, land and animals, and finally *Adam*, the Hebrew name for "humanity." But humanity rebels and turns away, and so there are curses of brokenness, toil, and death.

And one of those curses is on Eve, the mother of humanity: "I will sharpen the pain of your pregnancy, and in pain you will give birth" (Gen. 3:16).

The miracle of life, the gift of sex, and the call to create will now come at a price. And until the modern era, the leading cause of death among women was childbirth.

So what is the scandal of the manger? That God didn't wipe it all out and start over, but by grace redeemed the curse through one of the ways it was manifest: childbirth.

That the God who hovered over the waters of chaos hovered over the water of a womb.

The One who created the cosmos became an embryo to recreate us.

What we see as producing shame, God sees as a path to salvation. So then, it is not enough that Jesus is *God with us*, but he also is *God one of us* to heal, redeem, restore . . . to fix all that humanity broke after he birthed us.

This is why, before the scandal of the cross, we pause to adore the scandal of the manger.

CHRIST WAS BORN. CHRIST HAS DIED. CHRIST IS RISEN. CHRIST WILL COME AGAIN!

Do You Know the Rest of the Story?

22

MATTHEW 1:18–25 | This is how Jesus the Messiah was born. His mother, Mary, was engaged to be married to Joseph. But before the marriage took place, while she was still a virgin, she became pregnant through the power of the Holy Spirit. Joseph, to whom she was engaged, was a righteous man and did not want to disgrace her publicly, so he decided to break the engagement quietly.

As he considered this, an angel of the Lord appeared to him in a dream. "Joseph, son of David," the angel said, "do not be afraid to take Mary as your wife. For the child within her was conceived by the Holy Spirit. And she will have a son, and you are to name him Jesus, for he will save his people from their sins."

All of this occurred to fulfill the Lord's message through his prophet:

> "Look! The virgin will conceive a child!
>   She will give birth to a son,
> and they will call him Immanuel,
>   which means 'God is with us.'"

When Joseph woke up, he did as the angel of the Lord commanded and took Mary as his wife. But he did not have sexual relations with her until her son was born. And Joseph named him Jesus.

Consider This

I know what you're thinking: *Isn't this the same scripture used to open the last chapter?*

Yes it is. Because as Paul Harvey used to say, it's time for the rest of the story.

Last chapter we looked at Mary. Today it's Joseph's role. When you think about it, Joseph gets next to nothing this time of year. There are no carols with him. The Baby Jesus, Mary, angels, shepherds, wise men . . . even lowing cows all get lyrics. But Joseph gets nothing.

So first, let's recap the situation: Joseph and Mary are betrothed, which in their culture was more akin to being married, just not yet fully consummated. A betrothal involved entire families from both sides, including transfers of money, property, and other legal obligations.

A bride becoming pregnant before the final marriage cere-mony would bring shame to both families. She would be the one considered guilty, so under the law there were two options for Mary. One, be sent back to her father's house, never to marry again. Two, be stoned to death while people quoted Scripture over her.

Our text today calls Joseph a "righteous man" who looks like he's going to quietly let Mary go, assumedly to return to her father's house. The text also says Joseph "consid-ered this" (v. 20); the Greek word here can also mean "to become angry."

So Joseph is understandably upset, but in this patriar-chal culture he wants to spare Mary and probably keep the shame out of the public and behind closed doors. But God has a different idea. The angel shows up and essentially says, "Don't break up. Stay married. You're in this together."

Why? Well, remember how we got here. Creation began with a marriage: "a man leaves his father and mother and is joined to his wife, and the two are united into one" (Gen. 2:24).

But later, mission failure takes what was mutual and destroys it: "And you will desire to control your husband, but he will rule over you" (Gen. 3:16).

But just like Mary with childbirth, God uses Joseph to help redeem the curse through one of the other ways it was manifest: marriage.

Joseph doesn't rule over her. He doesn't rescue her. He submits . . . to her and God. As Paul says in the intro to his famous marriage advice: "Submit to *one another* out of reverence for Christ" (Eph. 5:21, emphasis added).

When Joseph takes Mary home to meet his family in Bethlehem, the gospel of Luke says she's "obviously pregnant" (2:5). But in submission to each other, they will bear the shame of this scandal together, ushering in the marriage of heaven and earth.

Joseph probably knew the derogatory names people would give to this child born out of wedlock. But he is called Emmanuel: "God with us." And so the child who looks like he is born from sin and will bring shame to the house of David's ancestors, is instead the Son of David born to save the whole world from sin and shame.

To save us from our private sin behind closed doors. To save us from our private shame closed up in our hearts. To save us from public sins that everyone talks about, and the public shame where people stone others with words while quoting Bible verses.

The manger is the invitation to the good news that, no matter what our sin or shame, God so loved the world that he gave his one and only Son to save us.

And now you know the rest of the story.

CHRIST WAS BORN. CHRIST HAS DIED. CHRIST IS RISEN. CHRIST WILL COME AGAIN!

The Real War on Christmas

23

REVELATION 12:1–5 | Then I witnessed in heaven an event of great significance. I saw a woman clothed with the sun, with the moon beneath her feet, and a crown of twelve stars on her head. She was pregnant, and she cried out because of her labor pains and the agony of giving birth.

Then I witnessed in heaven another significant event. I saw a large red dragon with seven heads and ten horns, with seven crowns on his heads. His tail swept away one-third of the stars in the sky, and he threw them to the earth. He stood in front of the woman as she was about to give birth, ready to devour her baby as soon as it was born.

She gave birth to a son who was to rule all nations with an iron rod. And her child was snatched away from the dragon and was caught up to God and to his throne.

Consider This

When my middle daughter was five she had a foot-tall Darth Vader figure destroy Bethlehem in her Fisher-Price nativity scene set. Then she surrounded Vader with the animals, shepherds, wise men, Mary, and Joseph in front of the manger. I could almost hear him breathing, "Jesus . . . I am not your father."

It was not your typical nativity scene. Very violent and "dark side of the force," like today's text, where John describes the spiritual realm on Christmas morning.

In a sense, we've domesticated the nativity story, casting the scene as a cozy barnyard bed and breakfast. But John's vision shows the birth of Christ as a cosmic war story, with Satan going after Jesus at his birth.

Now Satan is someone we either pretend doesn't exist, or blame for every bad thing that happens (#DevilMadeMeDoIt). Neither is helpful, and I don't want to give the devil too much credit. But Scripture shows he is part of the story.

Later on, John writes,

> "Then there was war in heaven. Michael and his angels fought against the dragon and his angels. And the dragon lost the battle, and he and his angels were forced out of heaven. This great dragon—the ancient serpent called the devil, or Satan, the one deceiving the whole world—was thrown down to the earth with all his angels." (Rev. 12:7–9)

Jesus said, "I saw Satan fall from heaven like lightning!" (Luke 10:18).

Peter said: "Stay alert! Watch out for your great enemy, the devil. He prowls around like a roaring lion, looking for someone to devour. Stand firm against him, and be strong in your faith" (1 Peter 5:8–9).

And Paul reminds us:

> "Put on all of God's armor so that you will be able to stand firm against all strategies of the devil. For we are not fighting against flesh-and-blood enemies, but against evil rulers and authorities of the unseen world, against mighty powers in this dark world, and against evil spirits in the heavenly places." (Eph. 6:11–12)

Jesus in the manger is the light in the darkness. But when we see the darkness he's coming into, we have to recognize there is more going on behind the scenes. Pete Greig, in his book *Dirty Glory*, says:

> Satan's not particularly interested in sin. His primary objective has never been to tempt you into violating a particular set of rules. His number-one aim is simply to divert your attention away from Jesus. He'll use sin to do it, for sure. But he's equally able to use busyness, or shame, or pain, or religion . . . or an obsessive relationship, or a golf handicap, or a pay raise, or an illness to distract you from the Lord. Satan hates the fact that when we fix our eyes on Jesus, broken relationships get fixed, and when we love him with all our lives . . . then death itself can lose its sting.[20]

---

20. Pete Greig, *Dirty Glory: Go Where Your Best Prayers Take You* (Illinois: NavPress, 2016), 37.

This is the enemy who sold Adam and Eve the lie that led to humanity's mission failure. And this is the enemy who was going after Jesus at his birth . . . the birth to redeem the lie we all suffer under. The enemy didn't take it well then, and still doesn't now. I believe that's why Satan tries to distract us with smokescreens like the "Merry Christmas" versus "Happy Holidays" skirmish. It's an intentional tactic to take our eyes off the real battle.

This week, as Advent turns to the stable, we must still remember the clouds. Jesus' return is the final victory, but his birth is the transfer of power from darkness to light, to "on earth, as it is in heaven" (Matt. 6:10). This is not the domesticated, warm-fuzzy, live nativity scene version we're used to telling. This is God loving the world so much that he would not only give, but risk, his Son being born. That's why we take a season to get ready, because there really is a war on Christmas.

CHRIST WAS BORN. CHRIST HAS DIED. CHRIST IS RISEN. CHRIST WILL COME AGAIN!

24 Not a Silent Night

LUKE 2:1–7 NIV | In those days Caesar Augustus issued a decree that a census should be taken of the entire Roman world. (This was the first census that took place while

Quirinius was governor of Syria.) And everyone went to their own town to register.

So Joseph also went up from the town of Nazareth in Galilee to Judea, to Bethlehem the town of David, because he belonged to the house and line of David. He went there to register with Mary, who was pledged to be married to him and was expecting a child. While they were there, the time came for the baby to be born, and she gave birth to her firstborn, a son. She wrapped him in cloths and placed him in a manger, because there was no guest room available for them.

Consider This

The day we brought our first child home from the hospital, a "once in a century" ice storm rolled in and froze the entire city. Many folks lost power for days. We were lucky and didn't lose ours.

We had carefully coordinated friends and family being in town during and after the birth so we could have help, but also time to ourselves. But now the hotel was in the dark, and the flights and roads that were supposed to take them out of town were frozen to the ground.

By the time our daughter was three days old, seven souls crammed into our little home. The guest room, the baby's room, and the sofa were all claimed. And my wife—who had put together the perfect nursing chair location, changing table set-up, and series of DVDs to watch during late night feedings—was stuck in our back bedroom dealing with a baby pooping herself and having trouble nursing. All while an unexpected family reunion occupied the rest of the house.

And then, as we went to bed, our power finally went out. It was not a silent night.

When a very pregnant Mary and Joseph showed up in Bethlehem for the census, the rest of his family would have been there too. The Greek word here is *kataluma*, which means "the guest room of a house," not "hotel inn." The issue was not rude hotel managers leaving a poor pregnant girl out in the cold. The real story is that the whole family was in town, and every spot in the house was claimed.

And the stable? Not a barn out back. Stables were connected to the front of the house so animals could be kept safe in bad weather. Small square windows were often cut between the stable and the house, letting the animal's body heat warm the house. And a feeding trough, called a manger, would be cut into those little windows or into the walls.

The Scriptures never say Jesus was born in a barn, just that the guest room was full and he was laid in a manger.

So I have a theory:

From what I've witnessed, a lot of family crammed into one house right after a baby is born is a hive of well-meaning, but mostly useless people. And I can testify that large, Middle Eastern families mean well, but want to be up in your business for every little thing with advice, commands, and unsolicited help.

And don't forget, these are Mary's in-laws.

Part of me is confident the stable was the best place to get away. A sanctuary for a mother and her new baby, where the family couldn't bother her and his crying wouldn't bother them. It was sometimes a custom to use the stable as an extended guest room, which may have been the warmest place for a new baby. So the Baby Jesus and his mommy were probably warm, safe, and excessively cared for by lots of family.

But maybe the practical helps set up the theological.

Genesis begins with "In the beginning God created" (1:1).

As we saw early in Advent, John 1, Colossians 1, and Hebrews 1 all declare it was God, through Jesus, who created all things.

It was God, through Jesus, who spoke and created the heavens and the earth. It was God, through Jesus, who created the fish of the sea, the birds of the air, and the animals of the ground.

And it was God, through Jesus, who took the dirt of the ground, breathed into it the breath of life, and created *Adam*, the Hebrew word for "humanity." And humanity was with God through Jesus in the garden.

And so it was that creation began with God, through Jesus, surrounded by the animals and the human family. Now swaddled in a manger, God in Christ is again surrounded by family and animals. A new creation event is happening this night, in a trough for a crib, that will lead to all creation being born again.

The Christ who created us also humbled himself to death on a cross . . . but also to pooping himself and having trouble nursing.

The new Adam is born in Bethlehem, and God is with us again . . . starting in the same place each of us did.

SO COME, LET US ADORE HIM.

25 | Baby Steps

JOHN 3:13, 16–17 | No one has ever gone to heaven and returned. But the Son of Man has come down from heaven.

"For this is how God loved the world: He gave his one and only Son, so that everyone who believes in him will not perish but have eternal life. God sent his Son into the world not to judge the world, but to save the world through him."

Consider This

On September 12, 1962, President John F. Kennedy stood at Rice Stadium in Houston and gave his famous "Why Go to the Moon" speech: "We choose to go to the moon in this decade and do the other things, not because they are easy, but because they are hard."

They called it the "moon-shot," an ambitious vision to touch the heavens. Nothing like it had ever been done before, and would it even work? But if it did, it would change humanity forever.

Then, just seven years later, Neil Armstrong stood on the moon and said, "That's one small step for [a] man, one giant leap for mankind." And something as common as walking became something cosmic.

We started the season of Advent with:

> In the beginning God created the heavens and the earth. The earth was formless and empty, and darkness covered the deep waters. And the Spirit of God was hovering over the surface of the waters.
>
> Then God said, "Let there be light," and there was light. And God saw that the light was good. (Gen. 1:1–4)

And as we saw, the result was mission failure: humanity created in the image of the Father turned away in fear and rebellion, and all of creation still suffers. Floods. Cancer. Mass shootings. Sexual assault. Terrorism. War. Hunger. Anxiety. Depression. . . . This isn't the way it was supposed to be.

Advent was first about getting us ready for Jesus' return to earth in final victory. But to prepare for that return, we first must join him in his birth: an ambitious desire for heaven to touch earth again. Nothing like this has ever been done before.

Christmas is God's earth-shot. Literal baby steps for the Son of Man that are giant leaps for all humanity. Bringing together the common and the supernatural: making the ordinary holy. By becoming like one of us who also suffers abuse, rejection, assault, sickness, loneliness, hunger . . . it means he is with us, we are not alone in our darkness, and it will not always be this way.

Something else happened that day on the moon that is significant for our story today. Between landing on the moon and taking the first step, there was first communion. Copilot Buzz Aldrin brought a small pouch of consecrated bread and wine on board, and before the moon-walk, he celebrated Christ's body and blood beyond the Earth.[21]

> Because God's children are human beings—made of flesh and blood—the Son also became flesh and blood. For only as a human being could he die, and only by dying could he break the power of the devil, who had the power of death. Only in this way could he set free all who have lived their lives as slaves to the fear of dying. (Heb. 2:14–15)

This is the gospel and the mystery of our faith: Christ was born. Christ has died. Christ is risen. Christ will come again.

SO COME, LET US ADORE HIM.

26 Christmas in Mecca

PSALM 96:1–10 | Sing a new song to the LORD!
Let the whole earth sing to the Lord!
Sing to the LORD; praise his name.
Each day proclaim the good news that he saves.

---

21. Buzz Aldrin, "Guideposts Classics: Buzz Aldrin on Communion in Space," July 10, 2014, www.guideposts.org/better-living/life-advice/finding-life-purpose/guideposts-classics-buzz-aldrin-on-communion-in-space.

Publish his glorious deeds among the nations.
    Tell everyone about the amazing things he does.
Great is the LORD! He is most worthy of praise!
    He is to be feared above all gods.
The gods of other nations are mere idols,
    but the LORD made the heavens!
Honor and majesty surround him;
    strength and beauty fill his sanctuary.

O nations of the world, recognize the LORD;
    recognize that the LORD is glorious and strong.
Give to the LORD the glory he deserves!
    Bring your offering and come into his courts.
Worship the LORD in all his holy splendor.
    Let all the earth tremble before him.
Tell all the nations, "The LORD reigns!"
    The world stands firm and cannot be shaken.
    He will judge all peoples fairly.

Consider This

Several years ago, my family traveled on Christmas Eve to Amman, Jordan, for a cousin's wedding on the day after Christmas. We all arrived okay, but my mom's luggage went to Rome. So we spent Christmas Day at the Mecca Mall in Amman getting new clothes for my mom.

Mecca Mall was just like any mall in suburban Dallas, with crowded stores during the holidays . . . especially because there were two holidays. That year, the Muslim celebration of Eid was the same week as Christmas, and Mecca Mall was decked out for the seasons. In the middle of the mall was a giant Eid display, complete with a huge replica Quran open to a significant verse hanging over a replica mosque set at the night of the new moon, surrounded by hanging strands of lights and fake lambs signifying the sacrifice for the feast.

And right next to all that was a giant Christmas tree, with a big star on top and lots of presents underneath, with a few plastic reindeer pulling a replica Santa sled up into the air.

All around the mall were signs in English and Arabic that read, "Share the joy of Eid and Christmas celebrations," and in the background I could make out "Jingle Bells" and "Silent Night" in Arabic playing over the mall speakers.

Here I was, in a majority Muslim country, and the Mecca Mall was wishing me a "Merry Christmas." To be honest, it confused all my notions of the so-called "War on Christmas" and all the cultural, political, and even spiritual emphases we place on it.

And then it made me wonder, *What story are we really telling in all this?* In America we decry the idol of consumerism at Christmas, while at the same time arguing about how much of Jesus should be wrapped up in what the salesperson says to us. And here I couldn't tell the difference between Mecca Mall and the Mall of America.

So what's the deal? As I said previously, I believe the whole "Merry Christmas" versus "Happy Holidays" skirmish is a smokescreen used by the enemy to distract us from what's really important. I believe one of the reasons we lose sight of the story we're supposed to be telling is because we miss that Christmas is a season, not a day (think "The Twelve Days of Christmas").

In fact, most of the Christmas stories we sing about during Advent happen *after* Jesus is born: angels and shepherds and rulers and killings and foreign visitors. What do those stories mean for us as followers of this newborn king? And what do they mean for a world of gods and idols?

Today is not the "day after Christmas." Today is the *second day* of Christmas. Just like Advent, we need a Christmas *season*, because the incarnation and its implications for the nations can't be fathomed in one day. In the birth of Christ, there are cultural, political, and spiritual stories at play that affect the whole world. We need to know these stories, and then tell them well . . . whether it's at Mecca Mall or the Mall of America.

SO COME, LET US ADORE HIM.

Angels We Have Heard Down Low

27

LUKE 2:8–14 | That night there were shepherds staying in the fields nearby, guarding their flocks of sheep. Suddenly, an angel of the Lord appeared among them, and the radiance of the Lord's glory surrounded them. They were terrified, but the angel reassured them. "Don't be afraid!" he said. "I bring you good news that will bring great joy to all people. The Savior— yes, the Messiah, the Lord—has been born today in Bethlehem, the city of David! And you will recognize him by this sign: You will find a baby wrapped snugly in strips of cloth, lying in a manger."

Suddenly, the angel was joined by a vast host of others—the armies of heaven—praising God and saying,

"Glory to God in highest heaven,
and peace on earth to those with whom God is pleased."

Consider This

My grandmother would set up her olive-wood nativity— the one she had picked up in a West Bank tourist trap—on the hutch next to the kitchen table. On the shelf above the manger, she would set six porcelain angels, each with a soft face, flowing wings, and either a harp or a trumpet. They looked like the house band for the Baby Jesus background soundtrack.

That's the image I think most of us have when we read the scripture above: benevolent celestial beings traveling from heaven to be, well . . . benevolent. But what if there's more happening here?

In his commentary on the gospel of John, Ben Witherington says, "The Son did not arrive here by descending through the Milky Way galaxy and turning left at Earth's moon . . .

Heaven must be seen as a parallel and presumably nonmaterial dimension of reality, not part of the material universe."[22]

In other words, heaven is not some fixed point in outer space, but a dimension on the other side of the veil from our world. Sometimes we forget there is an unseen spiritual reality to our Christmas story. After all, when it comes to the War on Christmas, our battle is "not fighting against flesh-and-blood enemies, but against evil rulers and authorities of the unseen world, against mighty powers in this dark world, and against evil spirits in the heavenly places" (Eph. 6:12).

That's why the angels are here. Think about all they've seen between both worlds from the beginning of the story until this moment. Some of what the angels were a part of include:

- Being at creation where, "all the angels shouted for joy" (Job 38:4–7).
- Fighting the war in heaven where, "Michael and his angels fought against the dragon and his angels" (Rev. 12:7).
- Watching Adam and Eve fall, and then after they were banished, "God stationed mighty cherubim to the east of the Garden of Eden" (Gen. 3:24).
- Witnessing the broken-heartedness of Hagar when she was mistreated by Abraham and Sarah, then coming to her rescue and saying, "Do not be afraid! God has heard the boy crying . . . [and] will make a great nation from his descendants" (Gen. 21:17–18).

---

22. Ben Witherington III, *John's Wisdom: A Commentary on the Fourth Gospel* (Louisville, KY: Westminster John Knox Press, 1995), 58.

- Passing over the land of Egypt, bringing death to, "all the firstborn sons in the land of Egypt," resulting in, "loud wailing . . . heard throughout the land of Egypt [because] there was not a single house where someone had not died" (Exod. 12:29–30).
- Worshiping in the throne room of heaven when Isaiah approached, confessed his sin and the sin of his people, and then God asked, "Whom should I send as a messenger to this people? Who will go for us?" (Isa. 6:8).
- Answering Daniel's prayers by fighting demonic forces in an epic three-week battle: "Since the first day you began to pray for understanding and to humble yourself before your God, your request has been heard in heaven. I have come in answer to your prayer. But for twenty-one days the spirit prince of the kingdom of Persia blocked my way. Then Michael, one of the archangels, came to help me, and I left him there with the spirit prince of the kingdom of Persia" (Dan. 10:12–13).

They've been waiting for this moment, and their celebration crashed through the veil between worlds like revelers bursting through the walls of a New Year's house party. They're not sweetly singing on high; they're seriously partying down below.

The appearance of the angels is not a peaceful interlude, but good news revelry. The very ones who have been in the battles from both sides now know the game has changed forever. For all they've seen, the darkness and violence they've been a part of now has a Prince of Peace.

Of course this is good news bringing great joy to all people. If they're excited, we should be excited. That's why we need twelve days of Christmas to celebrate!

SO COME, LET US ADORE HIM.

Why We Need Shepherds

28

LUKE 2:15–20 | When the angels had returned to heaven, the shepherds said to each other, "Let's go to Bethlehem! Let's see this thing that has happened, which the Lord has told us about."

They hurried to the village and found Mary and Joseph. And there was the baby, lying in the manger. After seeing him, the shepherds told everyone what had happened and what the angel had said to them about this child. All who heard the shepherds' story were astonished, but Mary kept all these things in her heart and thought about them often. The shepherds went back to their flocks, glorifying and praising God for all they had heard and seen. It was just as the angel had told them.

Consider This

The lowly shepherds. Probably the greatest cast of supporting extras in the whole Christmas story. After all, they're the role four out of every five kids probably played in their church's Christmas pageant. But it's time to move the shepherds from supporting role to main characters.

Even in Jesus' day, shepherds did the grunt work. They had the job no one respected or wanted, but society needed someone to do.

This often supports the most common interpretation of why they were the first to hear the good news. God is intentionally identifying with the lowest and forgotten, giving the gospel to the poor and marginalized first.

That is true, but it's not the whole story. Why are these shepherds so excited that this baby is born? Because it's not just *who* heard the good news first, but *why* and *where*.

First, there is the connection to King David. Like the characters in today's text, David was a lowly, forgotten shepherd boy—the eighth son and runt of the litter—when God chose him to be king. He was from Bethlehem, and the promised Messiah was to be a descendant of the shepherd king from B-Town. In other words, he would be one of their own.

But to really get what's happening here, we need to go back to the beginning, to our mission failure in Eden. The first time blood is spilled to cover humanity's sin and shame is when Adam and Eve are "naked and ashamed," and so to cover them up "the Lord God made clothing from animal skins for Adam and his wife" (Gen. 3:21).

From then on, animals kept having their blood shed for us. All the burnt offerings on the altar in the temple: the cattle and sheep and goats and doves and pigeons.

And the lambs. The ones sacrificed at Passover to remember the lamb blood spilled to save God's people from slavery in Egypt.

Which brings us back to our story in Bethlehem. In Hebrew, Bethlehem means "house of bread," and in Arabic it means "house of meat." Why? Because Bethlehem was the town where the lambs for the Passover sacrifice were born and raised. So these aren't just any shepherds who helped keep people fed, these are *the shepherds* who helped keep people holy.

These were the very shepherds who had a job because we needed a messiah. I think somewhere they knew this news would impact them the most because if the Messiah was really born, they would eventually be out of a job. And they rejoiced. What does that tell us about their level of darkness and anticipation?

So the gospel first went out not just to the lowest in society, but to the ones it would first impact the most. But why is this good news and not just a fun fact? Because there are three big Jesus statements in the New Testament tied to this moment:

First, Jesus says, "Yes, I am the bread of life! Your ancestors ate manna in the wilderness, but they all died. Anyone who eats the bread from heaven, however, will never die. I am the living bread that came down from heaven. Anyone who eats this bread will live forever; and this bread, which I will offer so the world may live, is my flesh" (John 6:48–51).

Second, he says, "I am the good shepherd; I know my own sheep, and they know me, just as my Father knows me and I know the Father. So I sacrifice my life for the sheep" (John 10:14–15).

Third, John the Baptist declares, "Look! The Lamb of God who takes away the sin of the world!" (John 1:29).

This is a eucharistic moment. It was the Lamb of God from Bethlehem who, at the Passover meal of lamb from Bethlehem, took bread, broke it, gave it to his disciples and said, "This is my body, given for you. Do this to remember me." Then he took the cup of wine and said, "This is my blood of the new covenant, poured out for many for the forgiveness of sins" (see Matthew 26:26–28).

And so, the One born in the "house of bread" will one day eat this meal with us again in the house of our Heavenly Father.

The good news is that God is intentional in all things. No part of the story is frivolous, and no person has just a bit role. And every time we eat our Lord's Supper, we can remember that Jesus didn't just die for our sins but was also born for them.

SO COME, LET US ADORE HIM.

Jesus' Baby Book Moment

29

LUKE 2:21–24 | Eight days later, when the baby was circumcised, he was named Jesus, the name given him by the angel even before he was conceived.

Then it was time for their purification offering, as required by the law of Moses after the birth of a child; so his parents took him to Jerusalem to present him to the Lord. The law of the Lord says, "If a woman's first child is a boy, he must be dedicated to the LORD." So they offered the sacrifice required in the law of the Lord—"either a pair of turtledoves or two young pigeons."

Consider This

The lives of my three daughters are very well-documented. Even before they were born, my wife and I were posting ultrasound pictures on Facebook. Literally thousands of iPhone pictures, videos, and Instagram posts later, no moment in their life seems left out (and I'm sure they'll thank us for all this someday).

But they don't have the one thing I do: a baby book. A tangible record of the photos, cards, clippings, and handwritten milestones my mother kept of my first few years. In a baby book, there's only so much space, so only the big moments make it to look back on later.

The first two chapters of Luke's gospel could be considered Jesus' baby book. And today's text is one of those really big moments that usually doesn't make the Christmas pageant.

Joseph and Mary have taken Jesus to the temple in Jerusalem for a sacred event that would bring a lot of joy to first-time parents: dedicating their firstborn to the Lord. Like all Hebrew boys, Jesus was circumcised at eight days old as an outward sign that he was in the covenant of Abraham.

Then he was officially named, and names were more than just titles in the Bible. Your name was also considered part of your nature. Names said something about your character and identity, and they were traditionally given by the father.

Then came the sacrifice. Having lost blood at birth and so considered unclean, Mary was required to bring a lamb and a dove for a sacrifice of purification. The lamb was for the burnt offering atoning for sin, and the dove was for the purification offering.

Luke only says that she brought two doves, and that gives something away. If the mother couldn't afford a lamb, the Law said she could bring two doves instead.

The common interpretation says this shows Jesus and his family were poor, another sign of God identifying with the marginalized first. That is true, but like we saw previously, there's more to the story . . . and it's all about identity.

One chapter later Jesus is grown:

> One day when the crowds were being baptized, Jesus himself was baptized. As he was praying, the heavens opened, and the Holy Spirit, in bodily form, descended

on him like a dove. And a voice from heaven said, "You are my dearly loved Son, and you bring me great joy." (Luke 3:21–22)

Do you see it? At Jesus' baptism the purifying Holy Spirit came down like a dove, and the Heavenly Father publicly declared the identity of Jesus as his dearly loved Son. Like we saw in the last chapter, God is intentional in all things. No part of the story is frivolous, and so Jesus in the temple sets up Jesus in the Jordan.

We've got a covenant, a dove, and a naming.

Now consider this:

When you came to Christ, you were "circumcised," but not by a physical procedure. Christ performed a spiritual circumcision—the cutting away of your sinful nature. For you were buried with Christ when you were baptized. And with him you were raised to new life because you trusted the mighty power of God, who raised Christ from the dead. (Col. 2:11–12)

Baptism is all about identity. It is a sign that we are in the new covenant because the Lamb of God was sacrificed to atone for our sins.

It is a sign that we are being given a new nature through the work of the Holy Spirit.

It is a sign that our identity is now "God's dearly loved son or daughter," and we bring him great joy.

This is good news.

SO COME, LET US ADORE HIM.

30 God's Big Plan for Your Life

LUKE 2:25–32, 36–38 | At that time there was a man in Jerusalem named Simeon. He was righteous and devout and was eagerly waiting for the Messiah to come and rescue Israel. The Holy Spirit was upon him and had revealed to him that he would not die until he had seen the Lord's Messiah. That day the Spirit led him to the Temple. So when Mary and Joseph came to present the baby Jesus to the Lord as the law required, Simeon was there. He took the child in his arms and praised God, saying,

> "Sovereign Lord, now let your servant die in peace,
> as you have promised.
> I have seen your salvation,
> which you have prepared for all people.
> He is a light to reveal God to the nations,
> and he is the glory of your people Israel!" . . .

Anna, a prophet, was also there in the Temple. She was the daughter of Phanuel from the tribe of Asher, and she was very old. Her husband died when they had been married only seven years. Then she lived as a widow to the age of eighty-four. She never left the Temple but stayed there day and night, worshiping God with fasting and prayer. She came along just as Simeon was talking with Mary and Joseph, and she began praising God. She talked about the child to everyone who had been waiting expectantly for God to rescue Jerusalem.

Consider This

College was a dark season in my life. Though I was surrounded with great friends at a great school, I was secretly overwhelmed with anxiety, depression, and loneliness. As graduation loomed near, and all my other friends were making plans for internships, mission stints, graduate school, marriage, and/or full-time jobs, I was planning to move back in with my parents.

What didn't help was some version of the constant refrain I always heard in sermons and Bible studies: *What are your goals? What is your vision? Dream big dreams and watch what God will do with them. God has a big plan for your life.*

But what of my life? I had no goals or dreams. I had no significant other. I was not destined for exotic mission fields, crowds of adoring parishioners, or even gainful employment. Then, after months of wrestling with this, I knelt at the altar during a prayer service and let Jesus have it: "I'd love to give you my dreams and visions," I said, "if I had any. But you've kind of left me hanging here. I'm still waiting for any clue of your big plans for my life."

Then, in a rare moment of the voice of the Lord in the stillness, Jesus spoke: *I am your dream. I am your goal. Whatever you do, and whomever you're in relationship with, will flow from your relationship with me. Not the other way around.*

In other words, the big plan God has for my life is Jesus.

In today's text, there doesn't seem to be much about Simeon and Anna. Two elderly folks who spend their final days hanging around the temple. Simeon seems ready to die. Anna was widowed early, and so seems to have spent most of her life fasting and praying. We don't know anything else about them.

When Jesus, the descendant of King David, shows up in the temple—a place crowded with people waiting for the descendant of King David—no one notices.

Except for the two old prophets.

Why? Because the plan for their lives had always been Jesus. Whatever they did, and whomever they were in a relationship with, seems centered in the hope of the Messiah. And when Baby Jesus shows up, this old man and this old woman, in what appears to be their final acts, become the first public preachers of the good news.

The secret is not our ambition, but a life "hidden with Christ in God" (Col. 3:3). It doesn't matter if we command a huge crowd or live in exotic lands spreading the gospel, or are a grocery bagger or stay-at-home parent in a house we can't keep clean, the big plan for our life is Jesus. And then, no matter what we're doing, it'll preach. That's why, regardless of the circumstances, we "can do everything through Christ who gives [us] strength" (Phil. 4:13).

The great thing about the incarnation is that Jesus showed up as a baby like we all do. In the Scripture, it didn't seem to matter who they were or what they did—a peasant girl or a shepherd boy or a rich wise man or an old woman—God's plan for our Christmas heroes was Jesus. And that's the real gift of good news for us.

SO COME, LET US ADORE HIM.

Expect without Expecting

31

LUKE 2:41–52 | Every year Jesus' parents went to Jerusalem for the Passover festival. When Jesus was twelve years old, they attended the festival as usual. After the celebration was over, they started home to Nazareth, but Jesus stayed behind in Jerusalem. His parents didn't miss him at first, because they assumed he was among the other travelers. But when he didn't show up that evening, they started looking for him among their relatives and friends.

When they couldn't find him, they went back to Jerusalem to search for him there. Three days later they finally discovered him in the Temple, sitting among the religious teachers, listening to them and asking questions. All who heard him were amazed at his understanding and his answers.

His parents didn't know what to think. "Son," his mother said to him, "why have you done this to us? Your father and I have been frantic, searching for you everywhere."

"But why did you need to search?" he asked. "Didn't you know that I must be in my Father's house?" But they didn't understand what he meant.

Then he returned to Nazareth with them and was obedient to them. And his mother stored all these things in her heart.

Jesus grew in wisdom and in stature and in favor with God and all the people.

Consider This

Before we leave the early temple stories, Luke jumps from preschool to preteen Jesus. My mother, who raised two boys, once said, "Do you know why the Bible only has one story from Jesus' adolescence? Because Mary didn't want to talk about it."

Passover was the big annual festival in Jerusalem, when the city would be overcrowded with out-of-towners making the pilgrimage. As a parent, I can empathize with the horror Mary and Joseph must have felt when they realized they had lost Jesus and had no idea where he was in that party-packed city.

Except he wasn't lost. He was right where he was supposed to be, in his Heavenly Father's house. Luke doesn't tell us what he was saying to the teachers in the temple. The details must not be important. What is important is Mary's dumb-founded classic mom question, "Son, . . . why have you done this to us?" (v. 48).

Mary stored this story in her heart, but I wonder at what level of ambition and anxiety. Joseph and she knew who Jesus was, but no one else did. "God, what have you gotten me into?" I can hear her asking.

When she got engaged, she didn't expect an unwed, virgin pregnancy. She expected to have children, but she didn't expect giving birth to the Son of God. She expected raising a son, but she didn't seem to expect to find him keeping pace with the temple teachers. What could she expect in the years to come?

That's the funny thing about expectations with God: we don't get what we're expecting. John the Baptist expected to see the Lord but didn't expect it to be his cousin. The people expected a Messiah, but they didn't expect he'd be from Nazareth. The disciples expected Jesus would conquer their enemies, but they didn't expect he'd win by losing on the cross. They expected he would establish his kingdom, but they didn't expect he'd do it by sending them out of Jerusalem.

We're still in the middle of Christmas, where we celebrate that the world expected a savior, but didn't expect him to show up as a baby. But on our wall calendar today is New Year's Eve, which begs the questions: What expectations do you have for this next year? What are your personal mission goals? What expectations do you have of God?

Maybe the key is to expect without expecting. That doesn't mean don't dream, don't plan, or don't work. But it does mean that we leave all the expectations of our ambitions and our anxieties in the home and hands of the Heavenly Father.

So let's end the year with the poem-prayer Jesus' great-plus grandfather, King David, wrote when he took the same pilgrimage to Jerusalem:

> GOD, I'm not trying to rule the roost,
>> I don't want to be king of the mountain.
> I haven't meddled where I have no business
>> or fantasized grandiose plans.
>
> I've kept my feet on the ground,
>> I've cultivated a quiet heart.
> Like a baby content in its mother's arms,
>> my soul is a baby content.
>
> Wait, Israel, for GOD. Wait with hope.
>> Hope now; hope always! (Ps. 131:1–3 MSG)

SO COME, LET US ADORE HIM.

What Christmas Can Teach Us about New Year's Resolutions

PHILIPPIANS 2:5–11 | You must have the same attitude that Christ Jesus had.

> Though he was God,
>> he did not think of equality with God
>> as something to cling to.
> Instead, he gave up his divine privileges;
>> he took the humble position of a slave
>> and was born as a human being.
> When he appeared in human form,
>> he humbled himself in obedience to God
>> and died a criminal's death on a cross.
>
> Therefore, God elevated him to the place of highest honor
>> and gave him the name above all other names,
> that at the name of Jesus every knee should bow,
>> in heaven and on earth and under the earth,
> and every tongue declare that Jesus Christ is Lord,
>> to the glory of God the Father.

Consider This

Just a reminder we're still in the season of Christmas. Today is the eighth day, but it's also New Year's Day. Today is the day all our resolutions kick in—all our goals for self-improvement, built around the ambitions of who we want to be, what is important to us, or what we want to accomplish. A resolution is defined as "a firm decision to do or not to do something."

Of course, at the end of one of the biggest food-fests of the year, from Thanksgiving to last night's party, most of us resolve to eat better and lose weight. Then, when Valentine's Day comes around and we realize we've lost our resolve, we look to Lent as "New Year's resolutions, take two."

We stay in this cycle, year after year, becoming more frustrated or discouraged. So maybe the place to start is not with our ambition, but our attitude. We need, as today's text says, the attitude of Christ.

We don't think of this as a Christmas passage, but take a moment and reread the first half of the text again.

This is about what Jesus did by becoming a baby. He emptied himself of all ambition and privilege. To be like Christ is not a resolution, but a reorientation. Resolutions are about working harder, doing more, trying to improve our old nature. Attitude is a settled way of thinking.

And the attitude of Christ is about giving up, to be raised up again.

So instead of a list of goals for the year, how about a prayer? A daily declaration of our desire to have the same attitude as Christ. John Wesley gave us such a prayer. It comes from his covenant renewal service, which was typically done on or around the new year, but is a prayer for the whole year:

> I am no longer my own, but yours. Put me to what you will, place me with whom you will. Put me to doing,

put me to suffering. Let me be put to work for you or set aside for you, praised for you or criticized for you. Let me be full, let me be empty. Let me have all things, let me have nothing. I freely and fully surrender all things to your hope and service. And now, O glorious and blessed God, Father, Son, and Holy Spirit, you are mine, and I am yours. So be it. And the covenant which I have made on earth, let it be confirmed in heaven. Amen.[23]

SO COME, LET US ADORE HIM.

Why Christmas Is a Political Movement

33

ISAIAH 9:5–7 NLT 1996 | In that day of peace, battle gear will no longer be issued. Never again will uniforms be blood-stained by war. All such equipment will be burned.

For a child is born to us, a son is given to us. And the government will rest on his shoulders. These will be his royal titles: Wonderful Counselor, Mighty God, Everlasting Father, Prince of Peace. His ever expanding, peaceful government will never end. He will rule forever with fairness and justice from the

---

23.   John Wesley, reprinted in *Watchnight: John Wesley's Covenant Renewal Service* (Franklin, TN: Seedbed, 2016).

throne of his ancestor David. The passionate commitment of the Lord Almighty will guarantee this!

Consider This

On election day 2016, a small group of us gathered at the statue of Francis Asbury in Washington, DC, to pray. We weren't praying for a particular outcome to the election, but rather for who God's people would be regardless of the vote.

I wrote down some of the prayers, which included:

God, we confess that we have left to the government the work of the church. We confess we've been more excited to talk about who we're voting for than about you.

Why were we there? Because of what happened at Christmas. We're taught not to mix religion and politics, but that's exactly how Luke begins the birth of Jesus story, with the Roman emperor Augustus. In his study on Luke, N. T. Wright points out that Caesar Augustus came to power through a bloody civil war, turned the Roman republic into an empire, and declared that he alone brought justice and peace to the whole world. He would be called savior, divine, lord, and "son of [a] god."[24]

Into this political reality, Jesus is born. The early church would make the political statement, "Jesus is Lord," which meant Caesar was not. But let's be honest . . . we struggle with this in our place and time. Every four years, half of us (statistically speaking) want to spike the ball in the electoral college

---

24. N. T. Wright, *Luke for Everyone* (Louisville, KY: Westminster John Knox Press, 2004).

end-zone, and the other half want to run for the Canadian hills. And with each cycle, we fall into the trap of believing if our candidate wins, there will be justice and peace to the whole world. For many of us, our tendency is to say, "Jesus is Lord, Caesar is not . . . as long as it's not my Caesar."

Scripture seems frustratingly inconsistent on the role of government and politicians. God uses a king and an army, but also says not to put your trust in them. Paul says to obey the governing authorities, but then rebels against them.

So how does the baby Jesus politically speak into all this? The root word for politics means "the public affairs of a people." And for God, all politics is global because he loved the world so much that Jesus was born. Throughout history, the work of God and the good news of Jesus has continued to move, whether Pharaoh, Emperor, Führer, Dictator, Dear Leader, Your Majesty, Prime Minister, or President is on the political throne.

Jesus is political, but not in the ways we think, practice, or post on Twitter. The government rests on a baby's shoulders because he's about the public affairs of a people from a place of humble incarnation, not hubris election. And his people are called to a radically different political campaign.

What does that look like? Well, let's go back to our election day prayers. Why is there even a statue of Francis Asbury on horseback in Washington, DC? Asbury was the first Methodist bishop to the United States, and on May 15, 1924, his statue was dedicated as the fifteenth rider to Washington. The previous fourteen were all military leaders. But this one was a missionary, and the celebration was not for the wars won, but the souls saved.

The dedication was given by President Calvin Coolidge, who declared that Asbury,

> did not come for political motives. Undoubtedly they were farthest from his mind. Others could look after public affairs. He was a loyal and peaceful subject of the Realm. He came to bring the gospel to the people, to bear witness to the truth and to follow it where so ever it might lead. Wherever men dwelt, whatever their condition, no matter how remote, no matter how destitute they might be, to him they were souls to be saved.[25]

The irony can't be lost that the government approved and dedicated a monument to a movement that government can't make. President Coolidge went on to say, "the real reforms which society in these days is seeking will come as a result of our religious convictions, or they will not come at all. Peace, justice, humanity, charity; these cannot be legislated into being. They are the result of a Divine Grace."

Because Jesus is Lord. Caesar is not.

SO COME, LET US ADORE HIM.

---

25. Calvin Coolidge, reprinted in *The Dedicatory Address of Calvin Coolidge at the Equestrian Statue of Francis Asbury* (Franklin, TN: Seedbed, 2016).

The Dark Side of Christmas

34

MATTHEW 2:16–18 | Herod was furious when he realized that the wise men had outwitted him. He sent soldiers to kill all the boys in and around Bethlehem who were two years old and under, based on the wise men's report of the star's first appearance. Herod's brutal action fulfilled what God had spoken through the prophet Jeremiah:

> "A cry was heard in Ramah—
> weeping and great mourning.
> Rachel weeps for her children,
> refusing to be comforted,
> for they are dead."

Consider This

Recently a friend asked me if I could justify that God's plan for Jesus' birth involved the murder of innocent children.

It's a fair question, especially since we don't really talk about this part of the story during the holidays. Our manger scenes have donkeys and a star and wise men, but no dead innocents. But there is a dark side to the Christmas story, and we have to look at it.

Herod was a terrible, Jabba the Hut sort of man. He was afraid another king would take his place, so in jealousy and fear he ordered the killing of children. But was murdering babies God's plan so the baby Jesus could bring us hope?

I'm going with no. God didn't ordain murder so Jesus could be born. Jesus was born because murder exists. Herod comes from the same place where all the evil and death we face comes from: the curse on humanity after Adam and Eve believed Satan's lie.

He lied because he's been after Jesus since the beginning, and we're the enemy's collateral damage. The real war is not on Christmas, it is on Christ. He is the one who created all this and sustains all this, so he is the one the enemy has always been after.

So what is the Christmas hope in all this darkness? I'll let C. S. Lewis have the last word today from *Mere Christianity*:

> Christianity [believes] that this universe is at war. But it does not think this is a war between independent powers. It thinks it is a civil war, a rebellion, and that we are living in a part of the universe occupied by the rebel.
>
> Enemy-occupied territory—that is what this world is. Christianity is the story of how the rightful king has landed, you might say landed in disguise, and is calling us all to take part in a great campaign of sabotage.[26]

SO COME, LET US ADORE HIM.

---

26. C. S. Lewis, *Mere Christianity* (New York: Simon & Schuster, 1996), 51.

What Does Your Favorite Christmas Story Say?

35

MATTHEW 2:13–15, 19–20 | After the wise men were gone, an angel of the Lord appeared to Joseph in a dream. "Get up! Flee to Egypt with the child and his mother," the angel said. "Stay there until I tell you to return, because Herod is going to search for the child to kill him."

That night Joseph left for Egypt with the child and Mary, his mother, and they stayed there until Herod's death. This fulfilled what the Lord had spoken through the prophet: "I called my Son out of Egypt." . . .

When Herod died, an angel of the Lord appeared in a dream to Joseph in Egypt. "Get up!" the angel said. "Take the child and his mother back to the land of Israel, because those who were trying to kill the child are dead."

Consider This

At just six years old, I knew what was in the big box. I couldn't wait. So when I woke up in the middle of the night, I figured it was a good time to open presents and tore off all the wrapping to my new Star Wars Death Star. Then I opened another box. Then I opened one of my little brother's. Then my father woke, mad as Darth Vader. It's the Christmas story my mom tells me every year.

Since Jesus' birth is the first Christmas, imagine the story his mom told him every year: *When you were born, they tried to kill you.*

I have three daughters, ages nine, seven, and three. So I'm certain the child Jesus would ask Mary over and over again, "Mommy, why did they try to kill me?"

As we saw previously, Jesus was born because death exists. Of course they were trying to kill Jesus, because violence and death is the fullest expression of the curse from our mission failure in Eden. After all, the first thing that happened in the story after Adam and Eve left the garden was a violent killing:

> Now Adam had sexual relations with his wife, Eve, and she became pregnant. When she gave birth to Cain, she said, "With the Lord's help, I have produced a man!" Later she gave birth to his brother and named him Abel.
>
> When they grew up, Abel became a shepherd, while Cain cultivated the ground. When it was time for the harvest, Cain presented some of his crops as a gift to the Lord. Abel also brought a gift—the best portions of the firstborn lambs from his flock. The Lord accepted Abel and his gift, but he did not accept Cain and his gift. This made Cain very angry, and he looked dejected.
>
> "Why are you so angry?" the Lord asked Cain. "Why do you look so dejected? You will be accepted if you do what is right. But if you refuse to do what is right, then

watch out! Sin is crouching at the door, eager to control you. But you must subdue it and be its master."

One day Cain suggested to his brother, "Let's go out into the fields." And while they were in the field, Cain attacked his brother, Abel, and killed him. (Gen. 4:1–8)

But it's not just murder. Violence means "a force used with the intention to hurt or damage someone." That includes everything from jealousy, passive-aggressiveness, gossip, and trolling, to physical abuse, dropping bombs, and ending a life. So, in one way or another, we all suffer under the curse Jesus was born to reverse.

Remember how we started Advent? Early on we asked how the arrival of Jesus is good news in dark places like Aleppo, where children know someone is trying to kill them.

Is the birth of Jesus good news for the daughter sitting next to her dying mother in hospice? For refugees forced from their homes and land? For the teenage girl trapped as a sex slave? For the lands decimated by consumption? For the father with depression trying every medication? For race relations? For the gunshot victim? For the pastor with a porn addiction?

All of these questions, and the thousands of others we could ask, are rooted in some form of violence . . . some form of sin and brokenness damaging humanity in a way that leads to spiritual and/or physical death.

But my friend Molly Just points out a connection I never noticed: Eve's firstborn son brought murder into the world when he killed his brother out of jealousy and anger. Now,

Mary's firstborn Son will reverse the curse by being murdered on the cross out of holy love.[27]

What do our stories tell about the reverse of the curse? As we come to the close of the Christmas season, God's people must be able to tell *why* the story of Jesus' birth is good news. And we must tell it well, beyond the season.

SO COME, LET US ADORE HIM.

36 The Gift That Keeps on Giving

JOHN 13:34–35 | So now I am giving you a new commandment: Love each other. Just as I have loved you, you should love each other. Your love for one another will prove to the world that you are my disciples.

Consider This

Christmas Day and my birthday are a mere thirty-four days apart. When I was a kid I leveraged this to my advantage. There was a limit to the cash value my parents were willing to spend on presents for both events. So I would always ask for one item way beyond that limit, like my first record player with dual-cassette and six-inch subwoofers. They would say

---

27. Molly Just, "Mary and Eve: A New Way of Looking at Advent," November 30, 2015, http://www.beadisciple.com/blog/mary-and-eve-a-new-way-of-looking-at-advent/.

no, then I would cut a deal that it would count as both my Christmas and birthday present.

They'd agree, and on Christmas I'd celebrate my big gift. But by the time my birthday rolled around five weeks later, my mom would say, "He can't not open something on his birthday," and so I'd get another present.

Christmas was the gift that kept on giving.

While this was a scam, the Christmas season is not. So what happens next? It's easy to move and forget the mission once the decorations are back in the boxes and gifts are either returned, exchanged, or have already found their way into a drawer, never to be seen again.

But this entire Advent and Christmas mission has really just been preparation for the gifts that keep on giving.

What's the first gift?

"For this is how God loved the world: He gave his one and only Son, so that everyone who believes in him will not perish but have eternal life" (John 3:16).

What's the gift that keeps on giving?

"We know what real love is because Jesus gave up his life for us. So we also ought to give up our lives for our brothers and sisters" (1 John 3:16).

J. D. Walt calls John 3:16 the first half of the gospel, and 1 John 3:16 the second half. And here's the ultimate mission goal: J. D. says that when the world sees us give our lives to the second half of the gospel, they'll believe the first half.[28]

SO COME, LET US ADORE HIM.

---

28. J. D. Walt, *This Is How We Know* (Franklin, TN: Seedbed, 2017).

37 A New Orbit

MATTHEW 2:1–2, 9–11 | Jesus was born in Bethlehem in Judea, during the reign of King Herod. About that time some wise men from eastern lands arrived in Jerusalem, asking, "Where is the newborn king of the Jews? We saw his star as it rose, and we have come to worship him." . . .

And the star they had seen in the east guided them to Bethlehem. It went ahead of them and stopped over the place where the child was. When they saw the star, they were filled with joy! They entered the house and saw the child with his mother, Mary, and they bowed down and worshiped him. Then they opened their treasure chests and gave him gifts of gold, frankincense, and myrrh.

Consider This

Every year we set up our little olive-wood nativity scene at one end of the fireplace mantle. We don't put the baby Jesus in the manger until Christmas Eve, and we set the wise men up at the other end. And every day, we move them a little bit closer and closer . . . until they arrive on January 6.

In our Christian calendar, and in the gospel story, they're the end of the Advent/Christmas season and the beginning of Epiphany: the presentation of Jesus to the world.

We don't pay much attention to the Magi, other than to give their role in the Christmas play to the three biggest boys in the church. They're positioned with the shepherds and animals, and we focus on the gifts they bring.

But there's more going on than gold, frankincense, and myrrh. The bigger story is why they're even in Bethlehem, and it may be one of the most important parts of the story of Jesus' birth.

To understand why they're here, we need to end where we began: in outer space. Remember where we started our Advent/Christmas journey? We said we needed a new way to see the whole earth. We needed a new orientation, one with Jesus setting the orbit of our lives. Theologically speaking, we first needed a "Google-Earth" view to fully embrace "for God so loved the *world* that he sent his only Son" (John 3:16, emphasis added).

Over the course of Advent and Christmas we worked our way down to ground level, but Epiphany is about looking outward again, to present Jesus to the rest of the world. And he's already gone ahead of us.

We call it prevenient grace: the grace of God that goes ahead of us. The belief that the holy love of Jesus is pursuing all people, guiding them to the heart of the Father through the power of the Holy Spirit . . . *even if they're not aware of it.* Put another way, it's God drawing us into the orbit of Christ.

How is that happening with our wise men? The Magi were Persian or Arab astronomers and astrologers who studied the orbits of the stars and the planets, looking to the heavens for meaning and signs, and as the psalmist says:

The heavens proclaim the glory of God.
>   The skies display his craftsmanship.
Day after day they continue to speak;
>   night after night they make him known.
They speak without a sound or word;
>   their voice is never heard.
Yet their message has gone throughout the earth,
>   and their words to all the world. (Ps. 19:1–4)

And what's most important was that the Magi were Gentiles, not Jews. They didn't worship the same deity, keep the same festivals, or practice the same holy days. But they saw something in the stars that went ahead of them, guiding them to the new king they needed to worship.

God pursued and led them in the midst of something they knew. They were looking to the heavens for wisdom, but what they didn't yet know was that wisdom is a Person who had come from heaven to earth. They were really looking for Jesus, even if they didn't know it.

This is of critical importance to the mission: Jesus gets into each person's story, even if they're not aware of it. Remember what Paul said?

Christ is the visible image of the invisible God.
>   He existed before anything was created and is
supreme over all creation,
for through him God created everything
>   in the heavenly realms and on earth.
He made the things we can see

and the things we can't see—
such as thrones, kingdoms, rulers, and authorities in
the unseen world.
Everything was created through him and for him.
He existed before anything else,
and he holds all creation together. (Col. 1:15–17)

That means everyone is created by Jesus, for Jesus, and exists in Jesus . . . *even if they're not aware of it!* This includes the immigrant, the Muslim, the atheist, the person from the other political party . . . everyone, *even if they're not aware of it.*

So if someone is looking for love, they're really looking for Jesus. If they're looking for truth, they're really looking for Jesus. If they're looking for peace, they're really looking for Jesus. It's just that they still haven't found what—or really Who—they're looking for.

So if these past thirty-six days have been mission preparation, then let's get ready for liftoff.

What does that mean for us as we come to the end of Christmas? It means that if Jesus is pursuing every person, we can only know what he's up to by *entering into another person's story through holy love.* It's an incarnation invitation. We don't want to miss this! This is our awakening—our new earth-shot!

It's time for liftoff. It's time for a new orbit. It's time for a new mission.

SO GO TELL THE STORY, AND TELL IT WELL.

Acknowledgments

There's a Norman Rockwell painting called "Behind Apollo 11" that shows the first astronauts to walk on the moon. Standing behind them are their back-up crew, scientists, engineers, government officials, launch-pad workers, and even the crew's wives. No one takes a small step—or giant leap—alone.

Much of this book comes from standing on the shoulders of many others who blazed trails before me. Portions of it also evolved from earlier forms that appeared in blog posts, the e-book *Leaving Behind "Left Behind,"* and from sermons and Bible studies at the University of Arkansas Wesley Foundation and the First United Methodist Church of Heath, Texas. I am grateful to both communities for being a proving ground for these devotions.

I am forever grateful to J. D. Walt for assigning me to the back-up Daily Text crew. I could not do this if he, along with Mark Benjamin, didn't push me almost every day to write and launch. Thanks for being my crew/band mates.

Thanks are also in order for the support team at Seedbed Mission Control, especially Micah Smith and Andrew Dragos for patiently showing me how to record and post the Daily Text "donuts"; Nick Perreault for making it look good; Jessie Green for getting it ready to launch; and Holly Jones and her crew for making sure I stayed on target. Mission patches for all of you.

Also, thanks to the crew from the late great Threshing Floor Podcast, whose Advent episodes inspired some of the daily posts: Chad Brooks, Joshua Toepper, and Drew Causey.

And to my wife, Jennifer, who is our family's steely-eyed missile woman, keeping the girls and me on mission. I love you.